Young Riders Guides

Caring for a Horse or Pony

Robert Owen and John Bullock

Beaver Books

First published in 1976 by
The Hamlyn Publishing Group Limited
London · New York · Sydney · Toronto

Astronaut House, Feltham, Middlesex, England

ISBN 0 600 38199 4

Printed in England by
Hazell Watson & Viney Limited, Aylesbury, Bucks
Set in Linotron Univers Light
Line drawings by Gwen Green and Michael Youens

Contents

Introduction

If you ride a horse or pony it is important to know how he should be looked after. Apart from the obvious need to be able to care for him, and make sure he remains fit and well enough to be ridden, it will also give you a much wider interest in the various facets of horsemanship, and enable you to learn more about the ways and habits of an animal which can give so much enjoyment.

Even if the horse or pony you ride, or may be lucky enough to own, is usually kept out at grass, there may be times when he will be brought into a stable, and it is as well for you to know how to look after him then. And remember that looking after a horse or pony properly can give a great deal of satisfaction.

In this book we have dealt with the principal facets of stable management in three sections: first a chapter on the stable itself – planning it, running it and stable routine; then a section dealing with the care of your horse or pony; and finally a chapter on tack and equipment and how to care for it. At the end is a useful glossary of terms to help you.

In looking after a horse or pony there are some basic principles which must be followed, but items such as stable routine can be varied to suit the needs of the individual, and of course the horse.

We have tried to give enough information to enable the reader to look after a horse properly, and to know what to do if anything goes wrong.

R. O.
J. B.

Acknowledgements

The photographs in this book were supplied by the following:

Anne Cumbers: back cover
Equestrian (Press and General) Services Limited: pages 10, 17, 24, 32, 34, 41, 43, 44, 45, 47, 48, 49, 50, 51, 57, 62, 63, 67, 68
Keystone Press Agency Limited: front cover
Photonews: page 36

The stable and equipment

Why were horses first stabled?

Anyone who has trudged across a muddy field in an effort to catch an unwilling horse or pony and then spent hours trying to make him look smart will know the answer to this question.

As soon as people started to take an interest in their own appearance, they also wanted their horses to look attractive, and developed a pride in the way in which they were turned out. They realised however that this was more difficult with an animal that was allowed to roam about all the year round.

A stable was the obvious answer because it not only provided protection in bad weather, it also ensured that the animal was always on hand when needed. By the careful control of food and exercise, a stabled horse could also be kept in really hard condition and ready for any strenuous work its owner might require it to do.

Loose boxes give freedom for a horse to look out.

What is a loose box and why is it the best form of stabling?

Although many horses and ponies are kept quite happily in stalls, loose boxes allow greater freedom, enabling them to lie down and rest more easily. They can roll at will, and get a certain amount of exercise by walking round the box.

The loose box must have good headroom, be reasonably large, and be free from any sharp objects which could cause injury.

Doors should be of the type which open in two parts enabling the upper portion to be hooked back so that the animal can look out. Special safety latches are necessary to prevent him from opening the doors, which must also be wide enough to prevent a horse being led from the stable from brushing against a door post and damaging not only itself but also the saddlery. All light fittings and switches should be of the safety variety.

Mangers need to be fixed securely to the wall and should be deep enough to prevent a horse from throwing out its food, but high enough to prevent it from becoming cast underneath.

Most owners use hay nets because they are easy to fill and cause less mess, but they should always be tied up at a height to give a natural feeding position, and prevent seeds and dust from getting into the horse's eyes

All stabled animals need plenty of fresh water, and the water buckets should be kept full.

What is the best form of stable flooring?

Various forms of flooring are used in stables, but it is essential to ensure that whatever material is used is of the non-slip variety. It should also be impervious to moisture, long wearing, and reasonably warm and comfortable for a horse lying down.

Although concrete is the material in most frequent use, it is not entirely satisfactory, although it has the benefit in most countries of being relatively cheap and easy to obtain. If concrete is used, the surface must always be roughened to enable a horse or pony to get a grip, and not to slip when getting up and down, otherwise injury can occur.

Stable bricks are the best solution, but they are expensive and unfortunately no longer in plentiful supply.

In order to ensure good drainage and prevent the bedding from becoming too wet, the stable floor should be made to slope slightly. Shallow channel-drains either just inside or just outside the stable doorway usually provide the most efficient type of runaway, and are easy to keep clean. They can be connected either to a soak-away or to the main drain in the stable yard.

Covered drains inside the stables are less efficient because they can become clogged by the bedding, and are consequently more difficult to maintain.

Why is ventilation so important?

Horses and ponies need plenty of fresh air if they are to keep really fit and free from coughs and colds. Animals kept in stables which are stuffy and badly ventilated because their owners have the mistaken idea that they are providing warmth, are usually those who easily become victims of seasonal ailments.

Horses don't like draughts, and everything should be done to block up cracks and badly fitting window frames. If the stable faces south, and the bottom portion of the door is high enough to exclude draughts, it is as well to leave the top of the stable door open day and night, all the year round.

All stables should have a window, not only to provide natural light, but also as a means of additional ventilation. The best type is the kind which opens inwards, so that fresh air is directed upwards towards the stable roof, and not directly on to the animal's back.

Warmth in cold weather should be provided by rugs, and an additional blanket in winter, particularly if the horse or pony is fully clipped.

What is the best form of bedding?

Some form of suitable bedding is necessary in any stall or stable, not only to prevent a horse's feet from becoming jarred from standing for long hours on a hard floor, but also to encourage it to stale freely, and to provide a comfortable bed when it lies down to rest.

Straw is usually looked upon as being the best bedding material, but owing to rising costs wood shavings, sawdust and peat are also being used. Good quality shavings are certainly better than poor quality and dusty straw.

A stable barrow, shovel, broom, stable fork with blunt points, a four-pronged fork and a dung skip will be needed for mucking out a stable containing straw bedding.

If shavings, sawdust or peat are used, a long handled wire rake and a pair of rubber gloves will also be required. It is important for the droppings to be removed frequently during the day to prevent them from being trodden into the bedding. The rubber gloves are very handy for this purpose. Every morning all the droppings and very wet bedding should be removed, and the surface raked level.

In the evening a clean layer should be spread over the floor of the box, and the underneath layer can be used to bank up the sides of the stable as an added protection when the horse lies down.

Every few weeks, according to the size of the horse or pony and the size of the stable, all the wet and soiled material should be dug out and replaced with fresh bedding.

Specially treated shredded paper is a relatively new form of bedding which has been tried quite successfully in some stables, and the mucking out process is very much the same as for wood shavings.

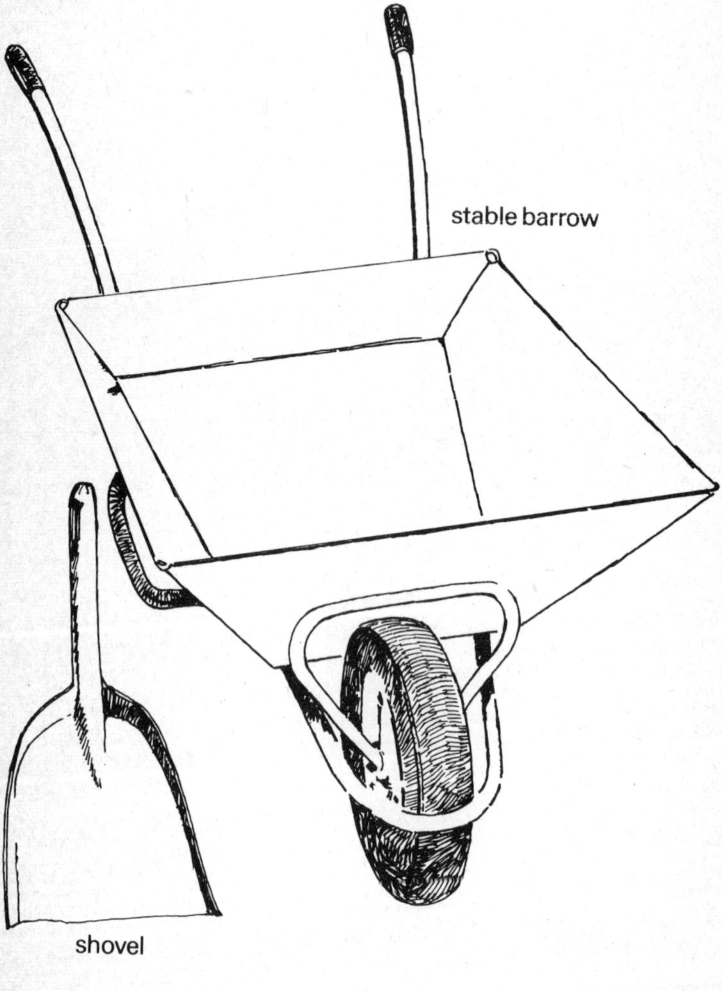

wire rake
broom
stable fork
dung skip
(plastic laundry
basket does
very well)
rubber
gloves
four-pronged fork

What is a normal stable routine?

The manner in which the various stable duties can be fitted into the work of the day must of course depend on whether there is someone looking after the horse full time, and the purpose for which it is being used.

Whatever decision is finally made regarding the daily timetable, it is important to remember that whereas horses and ponies get bored if they are exercised over the same route every day, they nevertheless do like to stick to a regular stable routine as far as is possible.

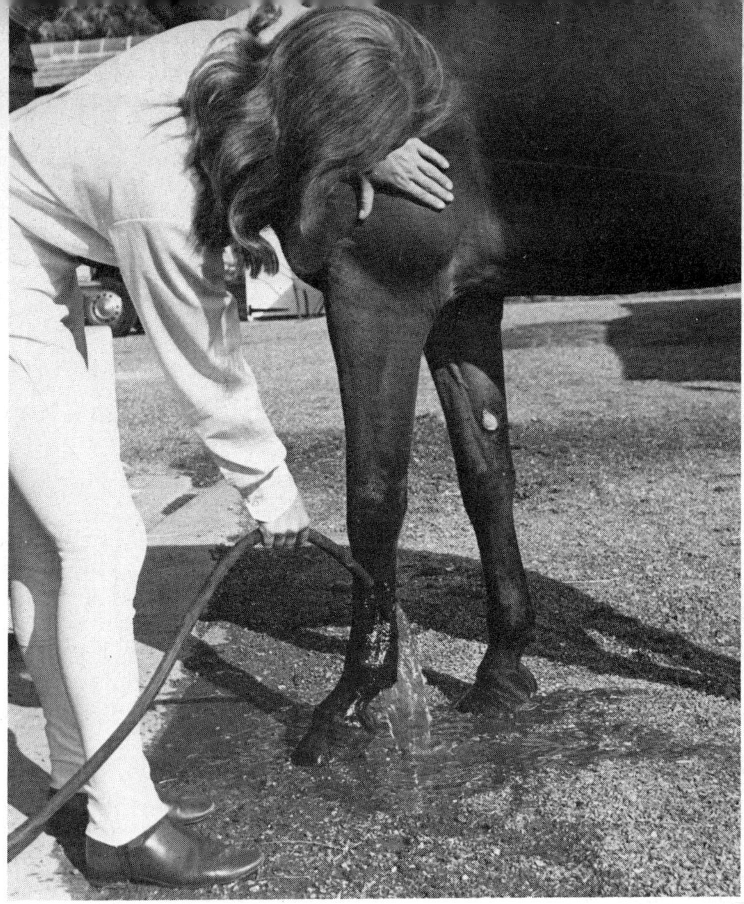

A horse with tendon trouble will benefit from having his legs hosed down after exercise on hard ground.

Horses and ponies, unlike their owners, always like an early start to the day, and if you are planning four feeds in the course of the day, it is as well to begin stables at about 6.30 a.m.

After tying him up with a headcollar, take a good look round to make sure your horse has not suffered any injury during the night. Then adjust the rugs, and make sure the water buckets are full.

A small net of hay will give him something to nibble, and keep him occupied while you muck out, and pick out his feet. The rugs should again be checked and he will then be ready for his first feed of the day at 7.30 a.m.

You must leave at least an hour between feed time and exercise, and this will give you time for your own breakfast and to check on the day's requirements.

At 9.0 a.m. you can remove his rugs, give him a quick brush over to remove any bits of bedding, and then tack him up for the morning's exercise. On returning to the stable take off his saddle and bridle, make sure he still has enough water, and allow him to stale. If you have been careful to walk the last part of the ride your horse should not be too hot, but if he is put on a sweat sheet and cover it with a light blanket and surcingle (see pages 41–6).

Now it's your turn for exercise. Tie him up and get to work to give him a thorough grooming while he is still warm. When you are satisfied with the results, and he begins to look ten times the horse he was when you started, put on his day rugs, refill the water bucket, let him loose and give him his second feed of the day. While he is eating this put up a full net of the best hay you can find and leave him to enjoy the next few hours to himself. There will be plenty of jobs for you to do around the stable and yard, and checking the state of the feed room.

At 4 p.m., if you really want to spoil your horse, take him in a titbit and make a fuss of him before tying him up and removing all the droppings and any damp bedding. Then pick out his feet into a dung skip, and bed down. Replace his day rug with the night rug, and a blanket if it's a cold winter night, refill the water buckets, untie him and remove his headcollar.

By 4.30 p.m. he will be ready for his third feed, and you should be ready for a tack cleaning session.

About 7.0 p.m. remove any droppings, refill his water buckets, tie up a full net of hay and give him his fourth and last feed.

Most important Last thing at night before you go to bed, slip quietly into the stables and make sure he is all right. It will be some hours before morning stables, and a last look round is always wise.

What is the ideal stable plan?

When planning a stable layout, the placing of various important areas must be considered – i.e., hay and straw barns, muck-heaps, fodder rooms and tack rooms.

Stables should preferably be within sight of the house so that the horses or ponies can be seen; essential extras like a fodder room and tack room can be incorporated to form windbreaks at either end of the stables.

Some form of hay and straw barns will also be needed but these should be placed to avoid any risk of fire. If large quantities of hay and straw are required the barns should be away from the main stable block.

Muck-heaps need to be placed somewhere handy to the stables, and an easy and firm approach for the muck lorry is essential.

Tack rooms need to be dry and secure, and apart from wall racks for the saddles and bridles, it is also important to have good storage for spare rugs, bandages, less frequently used tack, cleaning materials and if possible a sink with hot and cold running water. A table and saddle horse are also very useful.

Fodder rooms need to be within easy reach of the stables and they must be dry and vermin-proof. If you do get vermin, don't use rat poison which is highly dangerous to other animals and children. Ask for expert advice or better still keep a good stable cat. All foodstuff should be kept in vermin-proof bins, and plastic dustbins are excellent for this purpose.

A stable plan which shows a most practical and workable layout.

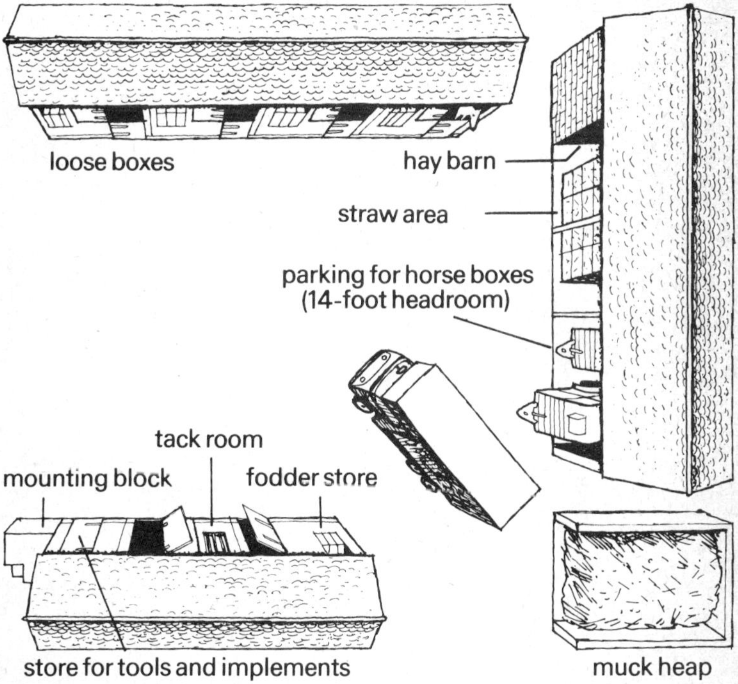

The care of the horse

Why is grooming important?

In his natural environment a horse would be able to roll and exercise at will, but if he is denied this freedom, his skin and feet can suffer unless he gets a thorough daily grooming. It should be remembered that the skin is as vital an organ to a horse's health as either his lungs or his heart.

Grooming has five main objectives: to promote health; to maintain condition; to prevent disease; to ensure cleanliness; and to improve appearance.

The grooming kit is consequently an essential part of every horse owner's equipment. A hoof pick is necessary for cleaning out the feet; a dandy brush will be needed for removing dirt and caked mud; the body brush will remove dust and scurf from the coat; and the steel curry comb will help keep the brush clean. A rubber curry comb is sometimes used along with the dandy brush to remove mud from the coat, particularly when a horse or pony has been out in the field. The water brush is important because when dampened it can lay the mane and tail, and clean the feet. A stable sponge will be necessary for cleaning the muzzle, eyes and dock, and a wisp will massage and promote the circulation. A stable rubber will provide a final polish.

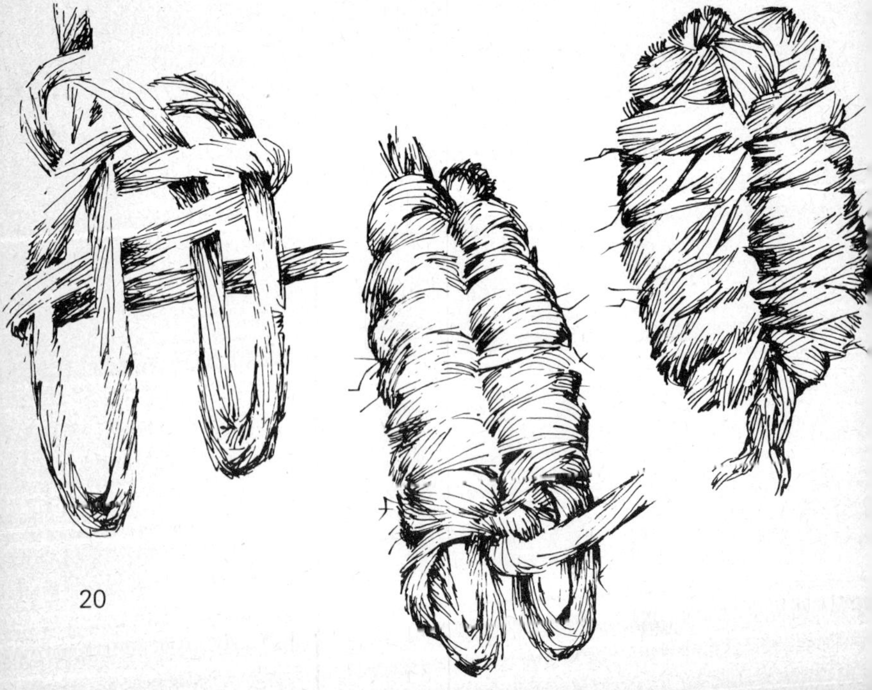

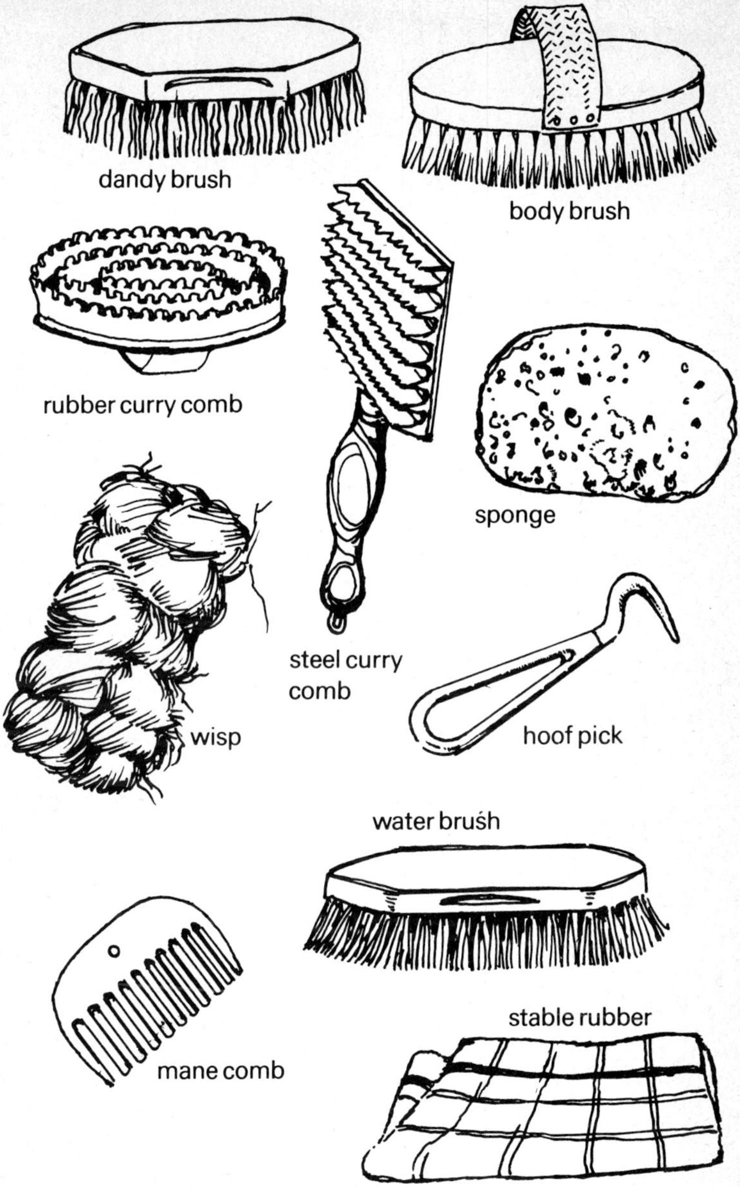
dandy brush
body brush
rubber curry comb
steel curry comb
sponge
wisp
hoof pick
water brush
mane comb
stable rubber

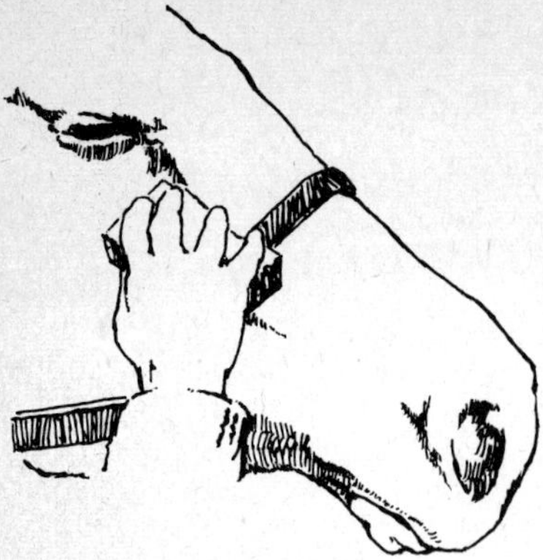

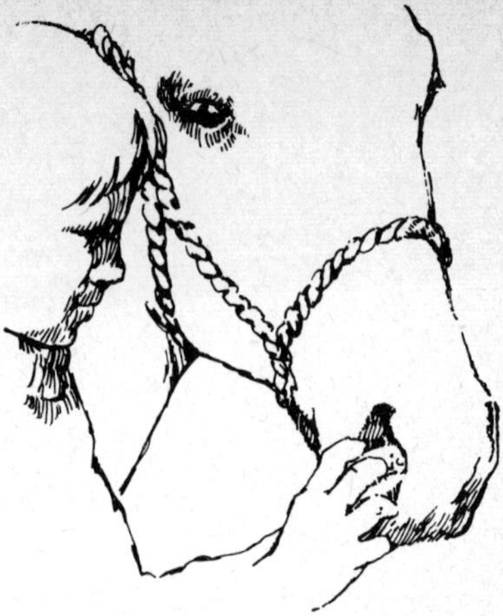

What is the importance of exercise?
A horse or pony in constant use needs sufficient exercise to keep him healthy and fit without causing him any undue exertion and loss of condition. If a horse is to maintain condition, exercise is essential.

When an animal is fat and has too big a belly, and his muscles are slack so that he is unable to do any fast work without sweating and showing signs of distress, he is said to be in 'soft' condition. He is looked upon as being in 'hard' condition when he is free of superfluous fat, and his muscles and tendons can withstand sustained effort without damage or distress.

It is important to know when your horse is really fit. The fat, round horse or pony at grass is likely to have soft and flabby muscles including those of his heart and lungs. His large belly will also occupy some of the space needed for his lungs to expand properly.

Once he is fit, however, the muscles of his limbs will be able to stand up to the strain of fast work without becoming tired, or worse still, breaking down. The muscles of his heart will be equal to the demands placed upon them, and those of his chest will help him to breathe fully and easily. The fat belly will have disappeared so that it will no longer be pressing on the chest to interfere with breathing, and the lungs will have greater space in which to work properly.

Two essentials are necessary to convert an animal from the soft to hard condition: sufficient food of the right kind, and the correct amount of the right work.

Slow steady exercise is important. Fast trotting and galloping will never get a horse or pony fit: indeed it will be more likely to do harm.

Once the animal is fit he will need regular exercise in order to keep him in 'hard' condition.

How would you feed a stabled horse or pony?

Grazing is of course the natural system of feeding, and grass is the horse's natural food. A horse in its natural environment will eat a little at a time throughout the day and night, and because of this it has a remarkably small stomach. That is why 'little and often' is the rule to remember when feeding a stabled horse or pony. The whole art of feeding properly is this adjustment so that the 'artificial' system of feeding comes as near as possible to the 'natural'. Always remember these basic rules:

1 Whenever it is practical to do so feed little and often.

2 Feed plenty of bulk food such as hay, so that the digestive organs have some food in them all the time.

3 Feed according to the work the horse is doing, particularly as far as concentrated foods like oats are concerned. If the horse or pony is doing a lot of work the amount of concentrates can be increased, but always be very careful when feeding oats to a pony. If the amount of work is reduced, feed less concentrates, but remember to compensate by feeding more bulk food like hay.

4 Always water before feeding otherwise the undigested food will be washed out of the stomach and all the goodness lost. It is better to keep fresh water in the stable all the time, and it won't matter then if the horse takes a short drink during or after its meal.

5 Try and feed something succulent every day to compensate for the loss of grass. Allowing a horse to graze for a few minutes can be very beneficial.

6 Because the stomach lies alongside the chest it can press on the lungs when full and restrict the breathing. For this reason a horse should never be exercised until at least an hour after it has finished its meal.

7 Never make any sudden change in diet. Any adjustment in the type of food or in the feeding routine should be made gradually over a number of days.

8 Only feed clean good-quality food. Feeding musty and dusty food will only lead to trouble and expensive vet's bills.

9 Keep to regular hours of feeding, not only because it is better for the horse's digestive system, but also because a horse looks forward to its food, and a disappointed horse will usually end up with a disappointed rider.

How would you clip and trim a horse or pony?

There are six main reasons for clipping a horse.

1 To enable it to do fast work without becoming unduly distressed.

2 To keep its condition by preventing undue sweating.

3 To enable grooming to be carried out more easily.

4 To help a horse to dry off more easily and quickly after fast work or exercise.

5 To allow a horse to work faster and better for longer.

6 To prevent disease.

A change in the horse's appearance usually occurs about September, when the coat appears to become dull and rough. The winter coat starts to grow, but it must be allowed time to become fully established before you think about giving your horse the first clip of the winter.

The first clip usually takes place about October, and, depending on the horse, the second clip should not be made after the beginning of January.

There are various types of clip:

The full clip In this clip the whole of the coat is removed.

The hunter clip Also a major clip, in that all the hair is removed, with exception that hair is left on the legs as far as the elbows and thighs, and a saddle patch is left on the back. The coat is left on the legs as a protection against cold, injury from thorns, mud, and cracked heels. The saddle patch is left to give protection against a sore or scalded back.

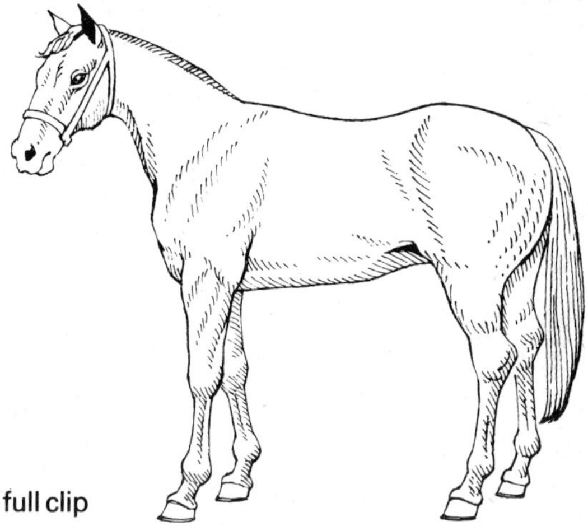

full clip

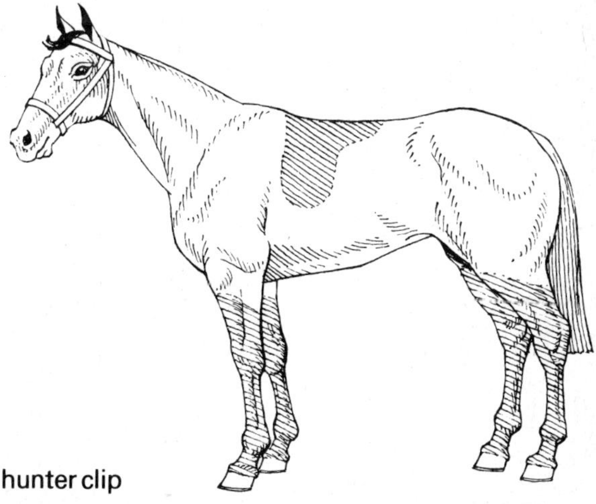

hunter clip

Sometimes hunters are clipped right out for the first clip of the season, but the hair is left on the legs and saddle patch for the second clip.

Anyone who is really skilled at clipping will be able to vary the position of the saddle patch to improve the appearance of a horse that may otherwise look short in the shoulder, or long in the back.

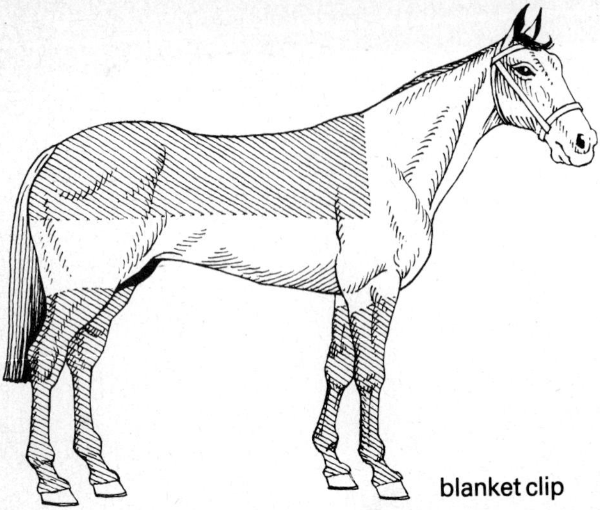

blanket clip

trace high clip

The blanket clip So named because the hair is removed from the neck and belly to enable the horse to keep cool during exercise, and the patch which is left is in the shape of a blanket.
The trace high clip This is a very handy clip for a horse left out at grass with a New Zealand rug. It is also a particularly useful clip for harness ponies. The hair is removed from beneath the neck, and also below the belly as far up as the traces, and from the legs as far as half-way down the forearm and thighs.

Before clipping can begin the horse's coat must be dry and reasonably well groomed. A twitch may be necessary if the horse gives a great deal of trouble, but patience and care are much more important, particularly with a young horse, or one which is not clipped regularly.

Hair must not be removed from the muzzle region or the ears, and care must also be taken not to clip the sides of the mane or the root of the tail. The clippers should not be used on the back of the tendons or the fetlocks.

A cold horse will become fidgety, and so it is as well to keep a rug across the loins, and if a hay net will keep him quiet, then it would be wise to give him one. Remember to move the comb and scissors upwards against the hair. Horse clippers must never be used on the tail.

The hairs of the mane and tail will need *trimming*, and they will pluck more easily when the skin is warm, and the pores are open after exercise.

Pulling is required to thin out an over-thick mane, or to reduce a long mane to the required length, so that it will lie flat. Hair should be removed a little at a time, and the longest hairs from underneath should be dealt with first. Scissors or clippers must never be used, and it is much better to pull the mane a little at a time, so that the horse does not become bored or restless.

When a mane is *hogged* all the hair is removed with the clippers. To hog correctly the horse's head needs to be lowered and the crest stretched, best done by an assistant standing in front of the horse's head and rubbing his ears until he contentedly lowers his head.

You should start by clipping the mane from the withers towards the poll, and care must be taken to make sure that no unsightly line is left where the coat meets the crest. A mane will usually need to be hogged every three weeks, and it is unlikely that a mane once hogged will ever become long again even after two or three years.

A *plaited* mane shows off the neck and crest; it looks neat, and also encourages the mane to fall on to the correct side, or offside, of the neck. There must always be an odd number of plaits along the neck, and one plait to even up the numbers on the forelock.

Some weeks after a horse has been clipped, long hairs known as 'cat hairs' will appear on various parts of the coat which will make him look rather untidy. The most usual method of removing these hairs is by *singeing*, but this task is best left to an expert.

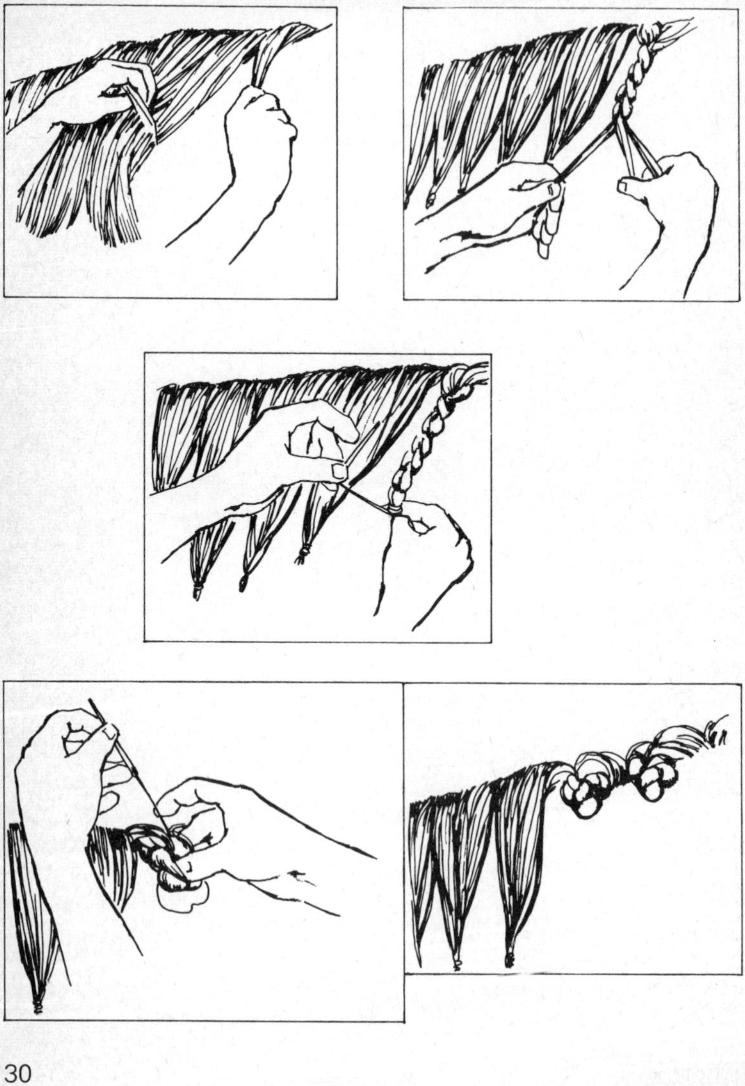

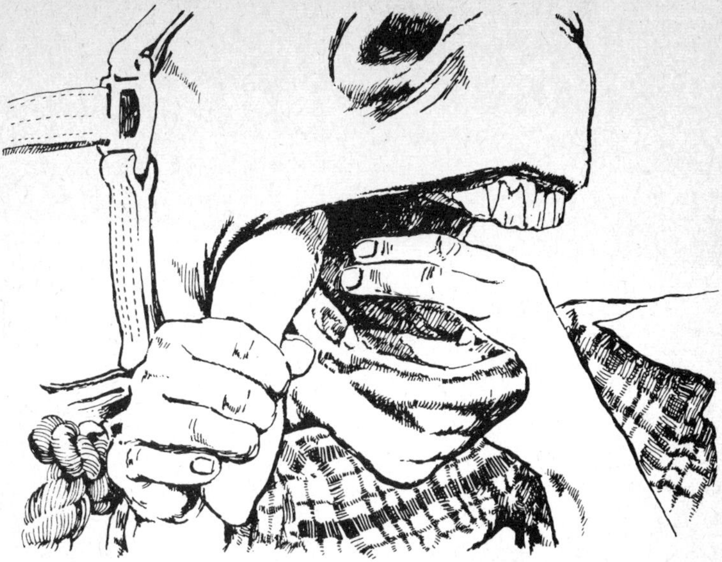

How should you care for a horse's teeth?

All horses need to have their teeth examined and filed at least once a year. A veterinary surgeon should examine them thoroughly for any sharp edges which might hurt the animal when he chews. To file a horse's teeth a gag is used to hold the mouth open, and to prevent the vet from being bitten. This is always a job for the expert.

The upper jaw is wider than the lower and the upper molars grow downwards and outwards, whereas in the lower jaw the teeth grow upwards and inwards. Because of this, the outer edges of the upper molars and the inner edges of the lower molars get little or no wear, so that they frequently become very sharp, and can cut the inside of a horse's cheek or the sides of his tongue. When this becomes particularly bad, a horse will not only refuse to eat but also begin to fight shy of his bit.

Care should be taken to make sure that a horse does not develop any wolf teeth which may require removing. They can be seen, or felt, just in front of the molars, and are small rudimentary teeth that sometimes appear after an animal is four years old. Besides being very painful they can also interfere with the bit.

It is surprising how many horses and ponies have their teeth neglected, so do take extra care with this aspect of your pony's health.

How is a horse shod?

A horse needs to be shod frequently, particularly if it has to do a considerable amount of roadwork, because otherwise the wall of the foot would wear away more quickly than it could be replaced. Even when shod, the wall will still continue to grow, and unless the shoes are removed, or replaced, at regular intervals, the wall will continue to grow until the foot becomes unduly long. The nails holding the shoe on to the foot will also become risen and these can cause cuts.

There are two systems of shoeing, *hot shoeing* and *cold shoeing*. In hot shoeing, the shoe is specially made by the blacksmith to fit the horse's foot and after being tried on hot and adjustments made until it fits perfectly, it is then cooled and nailed on securely. When a horse is cold shod, a ready-made shoe is fitted as well as possible.

Hot shoeing is obviously a far more satisfactory process, and there are six different stages – the removal of the old shoe, and the

The leather apron protects the blacksmith's legs as he drives the nails home to secure the shoe.

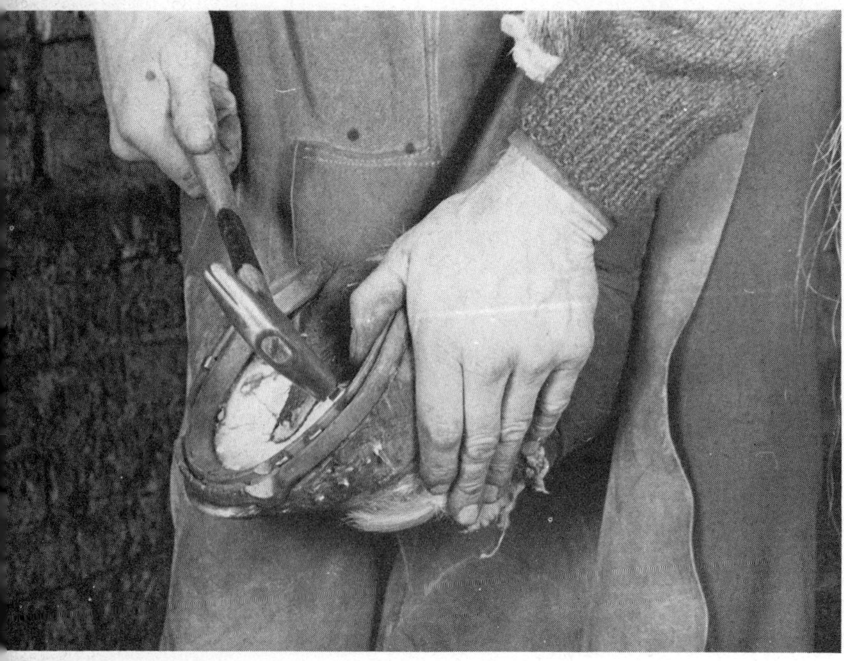

preparation, forging, fitting, nailing on, and finishing of the new.

When the blacksmith removes the old shoe, he first of all cuts all the clenches with the help of his buffer and driving hammer. He then levers the shoe off with his pincers, making sure that the wall of the foot is not damaged.

He then prepares the foot by cutting back any horn that has become overgrown, and making any adjustment of the hoof ready for the new shoe. The blacksmith cleans out the sole and frog, and makes sure that they are in good condition, and the foot is in good shape generally. Any wall that is not required is removed with a drawing knife or toeing knife or horn cutter. The rasp is then used to ensure that the foot has a level surface on which the weight of the horse can be borne.

The actual making of the new shoe is known as forging, and after the iron has been shaped, the nail holes are stamped and the clips drawn.

The fitting is carried out while the shoe is hot, and the blacksmith carries the shoe across to the horse on a 'pritchel'. By searing the horn he can make a perfect fit. This process is not at all painful to the horse, and if you watch a blacksmith at work you will see that although a horse will very often take a great deal of interest in what is going on, he never shows any signs of discomfort.

After the shoe has been cooled by being immersed in water, it is then nailed in place, and the end of the nail where it penetrates the wall is turned over and twisted off, leaving a small piece of nail projecting from the hoof which is called the clench.

The blacksmith nails the clips in position, and then finishes off by rasping the clenches smooth and imbedding them into the wall of the hoof. The rasp is finally run round the part where the horn and shoe meet, to reduce any possibility of the hoof cracking.

It is important to remember that a shoe should be made to fit the foot, and not the foot to fit the shoe.

There are various types of shoe, but the most common is known as the *hunter shoe*, which is ideally suited to a horse or pony doing fast work on grass, such as show jumping, eventing, showing and gymkhanas.

It is possible for a horse to work unshod, providing he does not have to work on hard gritty roads or flinty tracks, and every care is taken to ensure that the wall of the foot does not become too worn, so that he becomes footsore. The feet of a horse or pony working unshod will still need to receive regular attention from a blacksmith, not only to prevent splitting and cracking but also to ensure that the surface of the foot remains level.

How should you look after a horse's feet each day?

A horse's feet should be examined and cleaned out each day, because there can be few truer sayings than 'No foot, no horse'.

Pick up each foot in turn and remove any stones or dirt which may be lodged in the foot by using the point of the hoof pick, working downwards from the heel towards the toe. In this way there will be less chance of the pick damaging the soft parts of the frog in the centre of the hoof. Check by smell for any sign of problems like thrush, and run the tips of your fingers round the hoof to see whether there are any risen nails or clenches. Then tap the shoe to see whether it is secure, or whether a visit to the blacksmith may be necessary.

Always use the hoof pick from heel to toe.

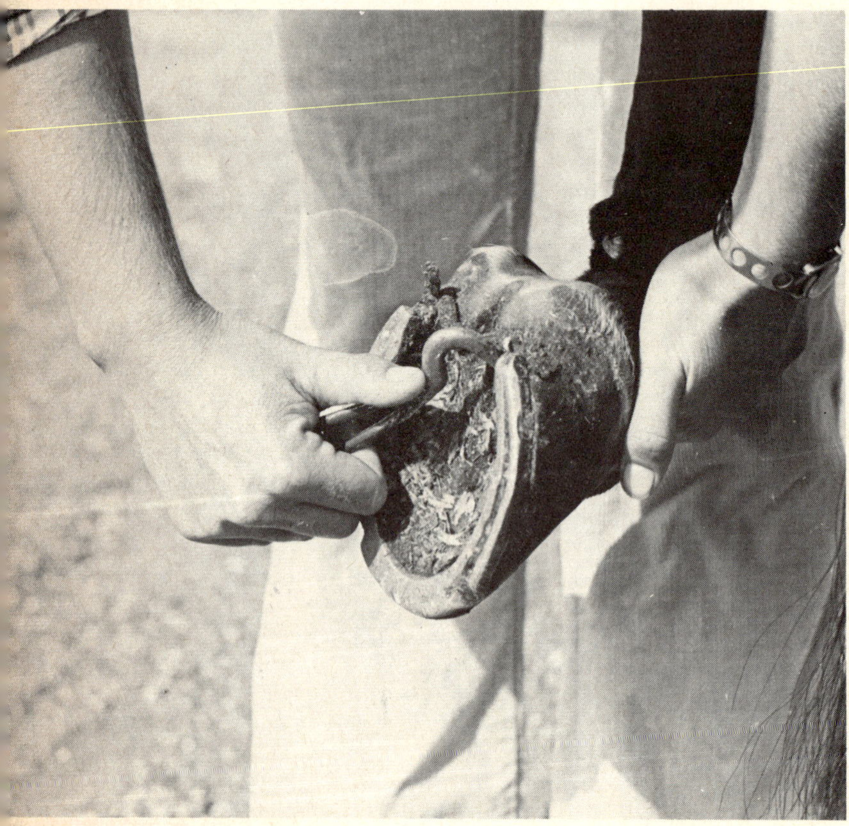

Picking up a horse's foot is not difficult providing you use the correct method. To pick up the off forefoot, stand by the horse's shoulder facing the tail, run your right hand down the forearm and take hold of the leg above the knee. Then exert pressure with your elbow until the horse's weight shifts to the opposite leg. Then lift up the leg with your left hand and take hold of the foot near the toe. The same method applies to the near forefoot.

When picking up a hind leg, stand facing the rear and run your hand down until it is just above the hock. Then take up the leg with the hand in front of the fetlock and lift the foot from the ground.

After cleaning out your horse's feet and checking the shoes, use a brush for a final oiling.

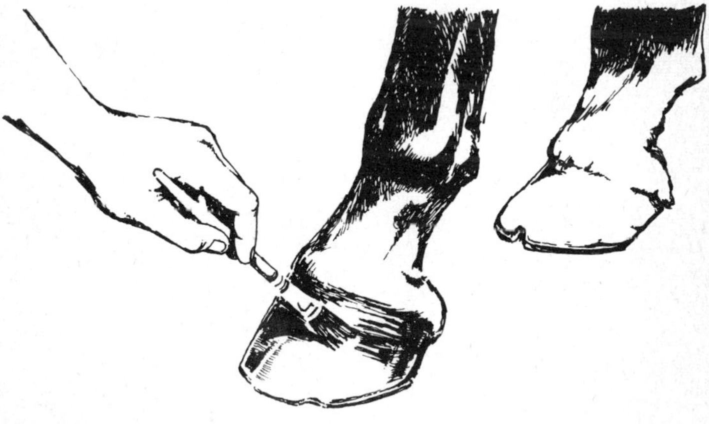

These two ponies look alert, bright-eyed and healthy.

What would you look for in a healthy horse?
A healthy horse should stand evenly on all four feet, with its forefeet square, its head up and alert, and eyes bright and wide open. Its coat should shine and the skin be soft and supple. If the coat is dull, or feels as though it is sticking to the muscles below; or if the hair is on end and not lying flat, then there is something amiss. A lot of discharge from the eye is also an indication that the horse is probably in a bad state of health. Droppings, which should be passed about eight times a day, should break on hitting the ground, and urine should be passed easily.

A horse never rests a foreleg unless there is something radically wrong, although a healthy horse will often rest a hind leg without any cause for alarm.

What would you do if you thought your horse was sick?

Like their owners, horses sometimes develop illnesses like a cold or even 'flu, and if you are worried about your horse the first thing to do is to take his temperature. The normal temperature of a horse is 38°C (100·5°F), but horses' temperatures are inclined to rise a little during the day, and it is often higher at mid-day than it is in the morning, or at night.

After taking his temperature, check his pulse. The general method is to place a finger beneath the horse's lower jaw where the heartbeats can usually easily be felt. Respirations in a healthy horse should be about ten to twelve to the minute, but should not exceed fifteen.

Any horse with a temperature or a cough, or who seems off-colour for no good reason, should be isolated if this is possible. If there is any doubt as to the cause of the trouble, or if he does not respond quickly to treatment, a veterinary surgeon should be called. Experience has shown that this is often cheaper in the long run, and there is less chance of your horse suffering permanent harm.

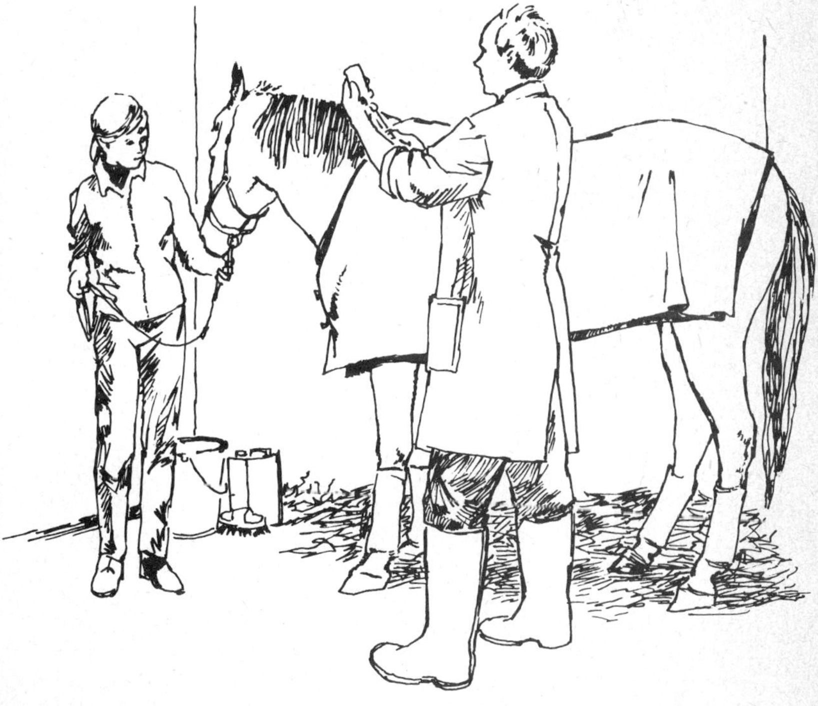

What minor ailments affect a horse's legs and feet?

In everyday stable life there are all sorts of minor ailments which come from the legs and feet. A frequent cause of lameness is corns, which are often caused by faulty shoeing. These are bruises to the fleshy sole between the hoof wall and the frog. If the bruise is very severe the foot may have to be poulticed, but if, as sometimes happens, the corn festers, and matter gathers in the heel, seek the advice of your veterinary surgeon.

There are many causes of lameness, from the less serious splints, which are bony growths on the cannon bone, to the very much more serious navicular disease; and from laminitis to bog spavins (see glossary).

A more frequent cause of trouble is the over-reach, which is caused by the foreleg being struck by the hind foot, causing a nasty wound either to the tendons or to the bulbs of the heels. This occurs usually when the horse is jumping, or it can happen at the gallop. The cut must be washed out with antiseptic and treated as for a bruised wound. This sort of wound can be entirely accidental or it can be caused through faulty action, or faulty shoeing behind, so it is as well to examine the hind feet. If necessary ask your farrier if he will round the inside of the hind shoes, and set them back as far as possible. If your horse is inclined to over-reach it is wise always to use over-reach boots for fast work and jumping to protect him from this type of injury.

Brushing wounds are caused by a horse striking the opposite leg on the inner part of the fetlock, or sometimes the coronet. The cause may again be bad action, ill-fitting shoes, bad conformation, old age, or even over-work. Once you have traced the cause, it may be as well to use brushing boots.

A stone lodged between the shoe and the frog can cause temporary lameness, but if the rider quickly dismounts and removes the stone there should not be any problem.

Bruised soles caused by a stone can take longer to cure. The sole becomes tender to pressure, and may show a red mark. A poultice or tubbing is usually the answer, as in the case of a pricked foot where a shoeing nail has actually penetrated the sensitive part of the foot after a visit to the blacksmith.

Cracked heels or chapping of the skin behind the pastern can cause severe lameness. They are caused by exposure to wet conditions, or neglect after the legs have been washed; you should always rub down your pony's legs after washing.

If the horse or pony is in a soft condition, girth galls can become a nuisance. They show on the soft skin behind the elbow. It is as well to leave the saddle off for a few days, and harden the skin by a daily application of salt and water or methylated spirit. A section of a rubber inner tube over the girth helps protect the sore from further rubbing.

How should a horse be given medicine?

There are six different ways of administering medicine to a horse. The simplest way is in the feed, but this is of little use if the horse is off his food. Whenever medicine in either liquid or powder form is administered in this way, the food should first be dampened.

Another easy way is in the drinking water, providing not only that

The modern way of worming is by means of a syringe, but this is not a job for the inexperienced.

the medicine will mix with water, but that the horse will be prepared to drink it.

The third method is on the tongue, but the medicine has to be mixed with something like treacle into a stiff paste, when it becomes known as *electuary*, so that it can be smeared with a smooth blunt stick either on the back of the tongue, or on the back teeth.

Horse balls, which are rather like pills or tablets, can be either blown down the throat or gently forced through the mouth with the horse's head raised. It is as well to massage the horse's neck when this is done.

Another popular way of administering medicine is by way of horse drinks. The horse's head has to be raised, and the medicine can then be administered slowly through the side of the mouth from the bottle. If he starts to cough, his head must be lowered immediately before the process can be repeated.

The other way of giving medicine is by means of an injection.

What is colic?

Colic, which is a pain in the stomach, is probably the most common of all horse ailments. It can be either a very mild attack, in which case it will pass off in an hour or two, or it can become very much more serious. It should never be treated in an off-hand fashion, because if it is not dealt with efficiently it can, and does, kill.

As soon as you realise that a horse has colic, telephone the veterinary surgeon immediately, because it may take him some time to reach the stable, and speed of action is important.

The first signs of colic are restlessness, so that the horse keeps getting up and down. He never wants to stay down for more than a minute or two at a time and when he stands up he keeps on looking around at his flank and trying to kick his own stomach. There are many other symptoms, but the moment you suspect that a horse is suffering from colic, keep the horse warm but walk him around, and try and prevent him from getting down on the ground and rolling.

Always try and find the cause of the colic, but usually it can be traced to bad stable management, such as watering after a feed; overeating when tired; feeding a horse poor quality food that might have gone off; sudden changes in diet; getting a horse chilled after fast work; leaving him in the stable when he is hot, or even neglecting to have a horse's teeth seen to regularly so that he is unable to masticate his food properly.

Saddlery and equipment

What are the most important rugs for a stable?

Every stable requires at least one rug, and if horses are stabled in winter, rugs and blankets will be necessary in order to maintain body warmth. There are many different rugs which are designed for different occasions.

When buying rugs it is important to get the correct size, and measurements are taken from the centre of the horse's chest to where the rug should reach on the horse's quarters. This is because the actual measurement size of the rug is the length from where the rug buckles in front to the back edge.

All rugs must fit comfortably at the withers and allow plenty of freedom of movement across the chest. The end of the rug should come within 10 cm (4 inches) of the horse's tail.

The Night rug is essential for a stabled horse in winter.

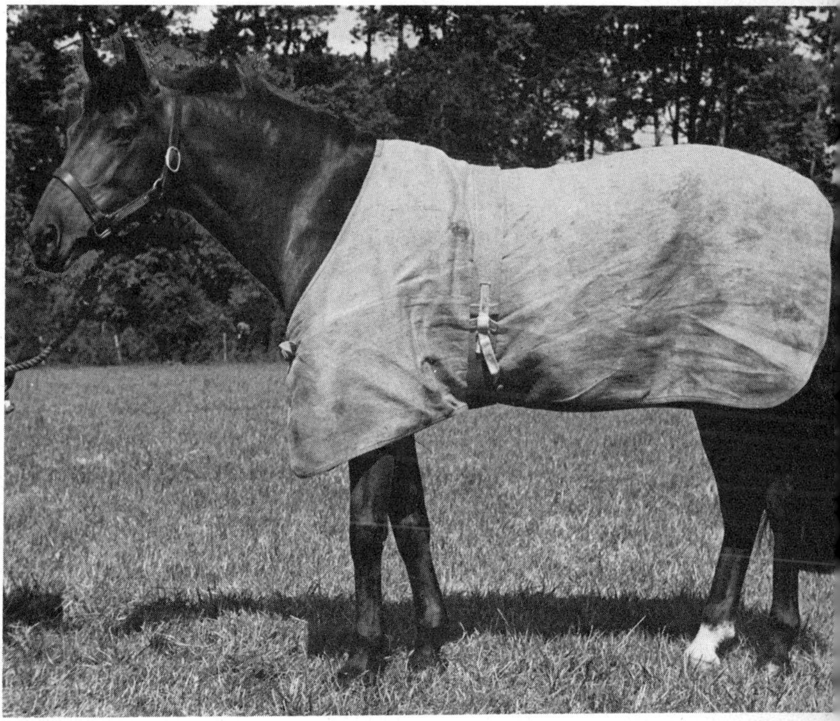

Night rug Of the different types of rugs, the most useful is the night rug or *stable rug*. This is made of strong jute or canvas and is lined with blanket. A good quality rug, if kept clean and repaired, will stand a great deal of wear and tear. Some rugs are lined at the withers, but if not, a piece of sheepskin sewn into the rug will prevent unnecessary rubbing.

In winter, when the weather is particularly cold, a good warm blanket will be needed under the rug. Good quality blankets can mean a saving in food, because if he is being kept warm by the blanket, a horse will not need to use up so much food in order to maintain body heat.

Day rug A woollen day rug with the owner's initials is perhaps rather a luxury, but it does look very smart, particularly when travelling or at shows. There are many qualities of rugging used for day rugs, and it pays to buy the best, because the poor quality rugs just do not last. Sometimes these rugs have a matching hood which covers the head and neck, and has coverings for the ears and holes in the front, cut out of the hood, for the horse to look through.

The day rug should be fitted with a *fillet string* at the rear to prevent the rug from blowing up in the wind. The fillet string is made of plaited braid to match the rug's binding, and it passes across the horse's quarters, beneath the tail, and just above the hocks.

Summer sheets These are made of either cotton or linen and take the place of day rugs during the summer months; like day rugs they can have the owner's initials sewn into the corners. The summer sheet is not intended to keep a horse warm, but to keep down the coat, and to keep away the dust and flies. It can be useful to keep draughts off the horse's loins when travelling, particularly when put over a string *sweat sheet*, and kept in place with a roller.

Lavenham nylon rugs and sheets These are becoming very popular for stable use because they are light and easily washed. They are made in a variety of colours and bindings and are fitted with a fillet string and surcingle.

Areborn rug A very useful item of stable equipment is the Areborn rug or *sweat sheet* which is rather like a string vest and works on the same principle, by keeping pockets of warm air between the horse's skin and the outer covering. It should be kept in place with a surcingle or roller, because horses when warm have a tendency to roll, and it is easy for them to get their legs caught up in the holes. It should always be used with another rug or sheet over the top because otherwise there is a very real chance of a horse becoming chilled across the loins.

The Day rug is made of wool and looks very smart.

Summer sheets keep away dust and flies.

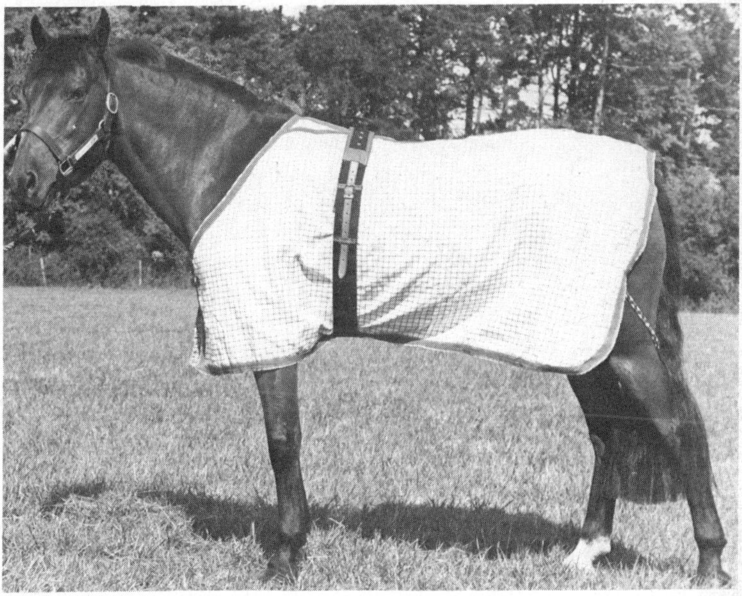

Lavenham rugs are light and easy to wash.

The sweat sheet is rather like a string vest.

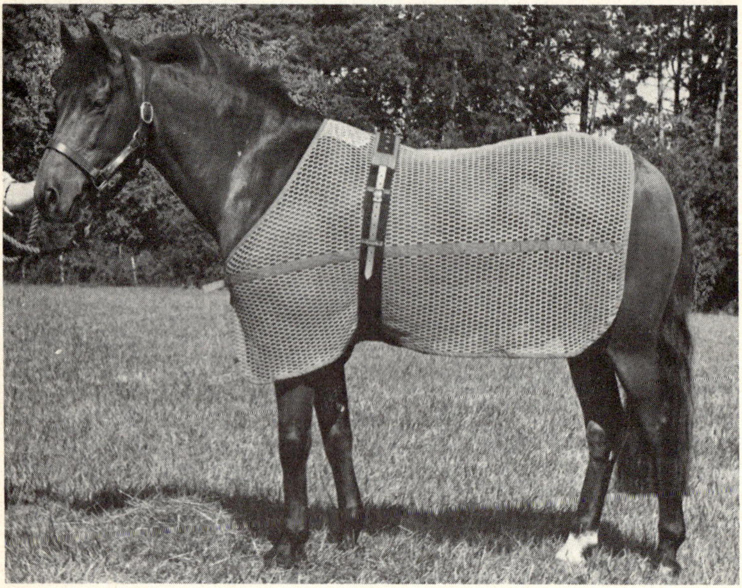

New Zealand rugs Although these are usually only used when horses or ponies are kept at grass all or part of the time during the winter, they are a very useful addition to the stable. Horses love being free to roll and nibble some grass even in winter, and in days when the weather is warm enough it can be very beneficial to a stable horse to be turned out for an hour or so with a New Zealand rug for protection.

These are waterproof rugs, usually made of canvas or nylon with leg straps that fasten round the hind legs to keep them in place when a horse gets down to roll. If a horse is turned out, the New Zealand rug must be removed and put on again at least once a day. The wither section of the rug should be padded for protection against chafing. When removing the rug it is important to unclip the leg straps first.

The art of 'rugging-up' is a skill which comes with practice, and is easily acquired if one knows the right way. Rugs and blankets are extremely expensive and it is worthwhile taking good care of them. There is no excuse for dirty rugs, although some staining is inevitable during the winter, or when a horse is stalled at night.

First unclip the leg straps of a New Zealand rug.

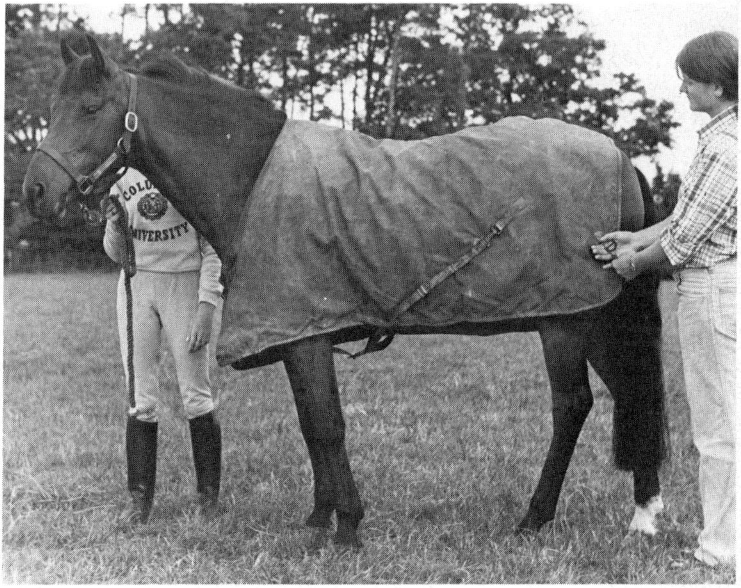

What is a surcingle and a roller?

Every rug needs some form of surcingle or roller in order to keep it in place. *Surcingles*, usually made of various types of webbing such as jute, wool, cotton or hemp, are long lengths of material with a leather strap at one end and a buckle at the other. Sometimes the surcingle is stitched to the rug, but it is important to ensure that it does not put undue pressure on the spine.

A *roller* is really a surcingle with a built-in pad that rests either side of the spine. Rollers are never sewn into a rug, and although they are fitted with their own padding it is as well to cut up a square of foam rubber to place between the withers and the roller.

If a *tail guard* is used the strap will have to be looped through the roller and buckled into place.

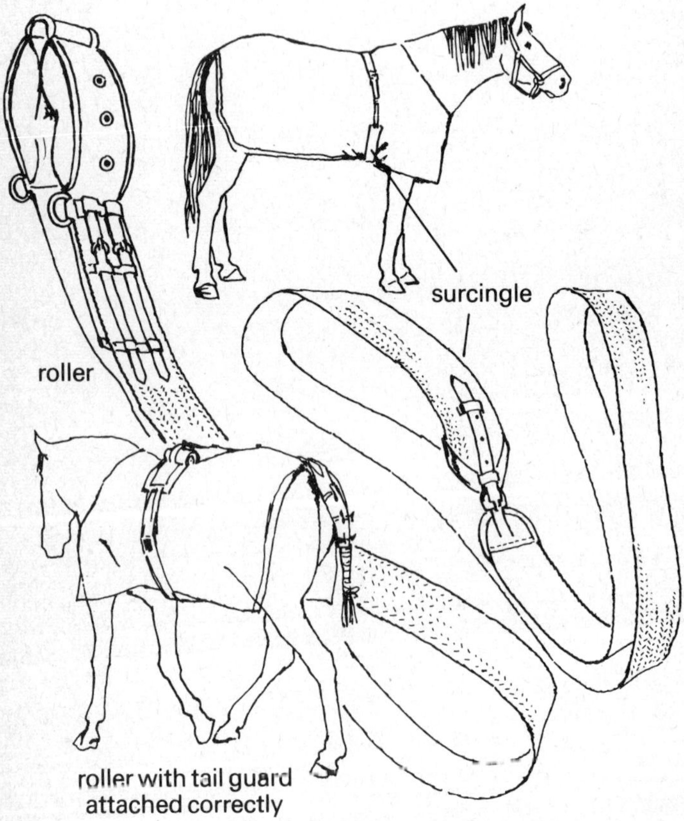

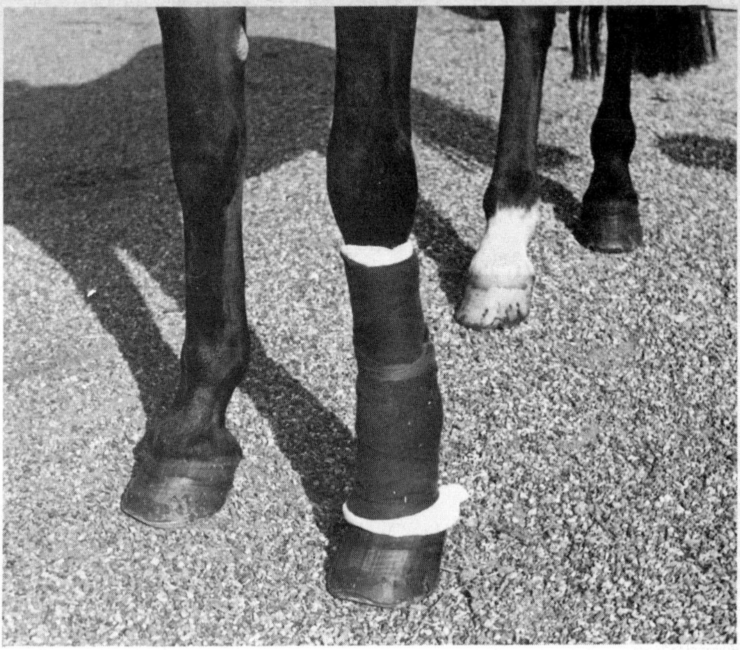

Stable bandages are made of wool and must not be tight.

What are the main stable bandages?

Bandages have a wide variety of uses apart from providing warmth and comfort. They can provide protection against injury when travelling, help prevent legs from filling, or help dry off wet legs, when put on over straw.

Stable bandages These are made of wool and must be carefully applied to prevent injury through being too tight. Before putting on a bandage make sure that it is correctly rolled with the tapes neatly folded up inside.

When putting on a stable bandage start just below the knee or hock, and pass the bandage round the leg in even turns. When the coronet is reached start to bandage again in an upward direction, so that the bandage ends at the starting point. The tapes should be tied so that the knots lie either to the inside or the outside of the leg, and not to the front where they will press on to the bone, or behind where they can press on to the tendons. The tapes should be tied in a double bow, and the ends tucked into the folds of the bandage.

Exercising bandages These are sometimes called pressure or support bandages; they are 6 to 7 cm ($2\frac{1}{2}$ to 3 inches) wide and made of stockinette or crepe. They are used to support the tendons at the back of the legs, to reinforce weak or strained tendons, and to protect the legs from thorns and brambles. Exercise bandages are applied with a considerable amount of firmness over a thick layer of cotton wool from just below the knee to just above the fetlock joint. Care must be taken, however, to ensure that they do not interfere with the action of the joint.

When the bandages are removed the back tendons and fetlocks should be given a brisk rub with the palms of the hands to ensure that the circulation is working properly. Never kneel to put on, or take off, bandages. A bending or crouching position is much safer.

Exercise or support bandages are used to support tendons and protect against thorns or brambles.

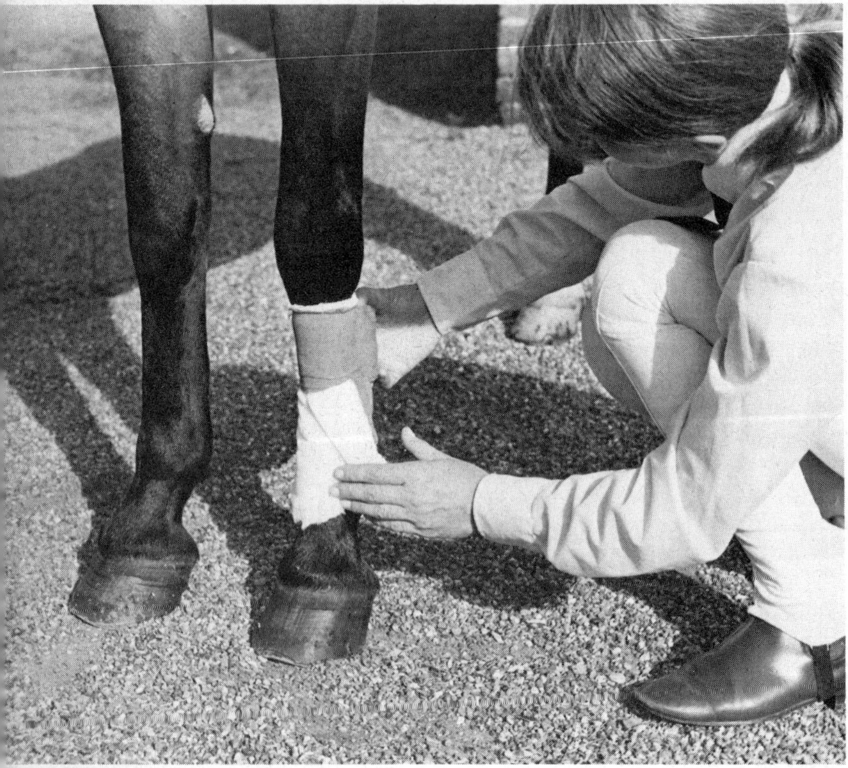

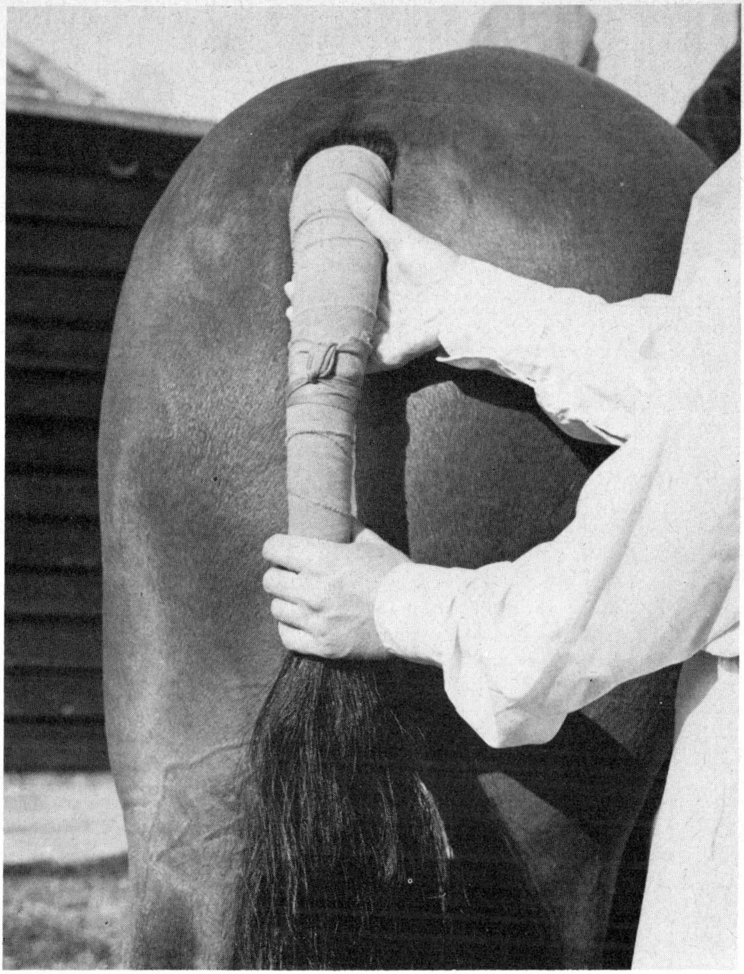

To remove a tail bandage grasp it very near the dock and slide it downwards off the tail.

Tail bandages Like exercising bandages, these are made of stockinette or crepe about 6 to 7 cm (2½ to 3 inches) wide. They are used to protect the tail from injury, or from being rubbed during travelling. They also improve the appearance of the tail and help keep the hairs in position.

Always remember that tail bandages should never be used too frequently, and must never be left on overnight. Before putting on a tail bandage dampen the hairs at the top of the tail with a water brush. Raise the tail with the left hand and, leaving about 20 cm (8 inches) of the end of the bandage loose, unroll the bandage evenly round the tail working slowly downwards. Secure the spare end, and when the bandage reaches about half-way down the tail start to work upwards again until the tapes can be tied neatly near the top, and tucked away under one of the folds.

To remove the tail bandage, grasp it firmly with both hands near the dock and slide it downwards off the tail.

Tie the tapes of the tail bandage neatly but only tightly enough to ensure firmness. The tail can then be bent into shape.

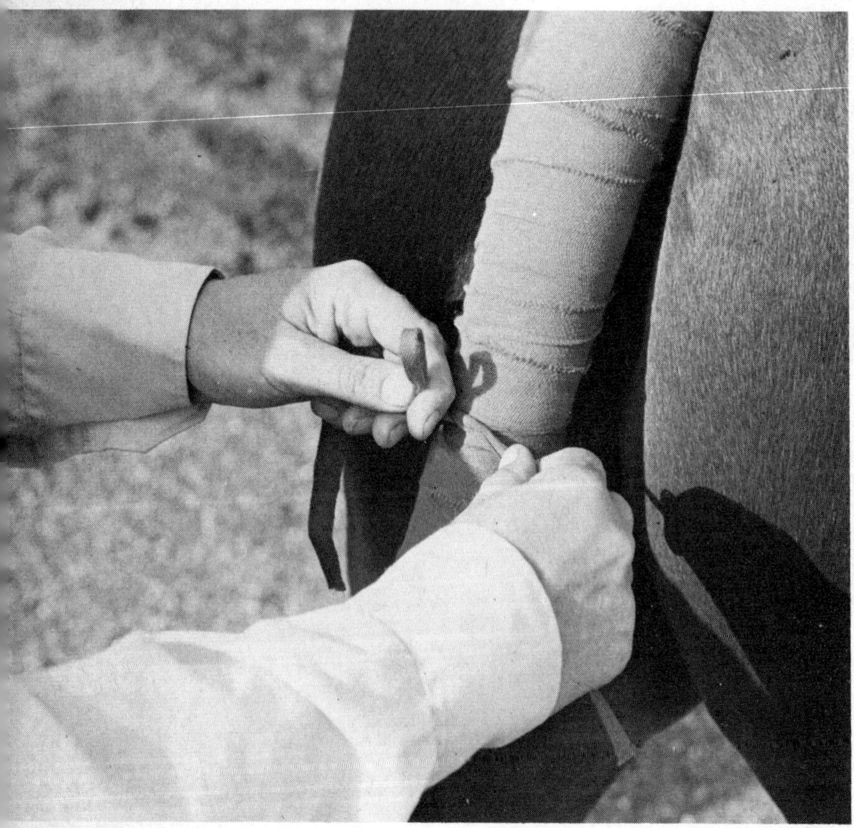

This hunting saddle gives security and comfort.

What should you look for in a saddle?

The saddle is obviously one of the most important items of equipment for every horseman and it is particularly important to ensure that it is not only a good fit for the horse but also comfortable for the rider. A saddle should be shaped so as to assist the rider to sit in the middle, or lowest part, of the seat of the saddle.

Saddles are built on frames called saddle-trees which are usually made of beech wood, but some saddles now have plastic trees. If the saddle becomes damaged, and the tree becomes broken, it must be repaired before the saddle is used again, because a saddle with a broken tree can injure a horse's back.

The stirrup leathers, which can be adjusted in length according to the rider's requirements, are fitted on to the saddle by being passed round a stirrup bar. This usually has a hinge with a point that can be turned up to prevent the leathers from slipping off the saddle when the horse is being led without a rider. It is important, however, to ensure that the points are never in the turned up position when the horse is being ridden.

Saddles are either full panelled or half panelled. A full panel is fully lined and reaches almost all the way to the bottom of the saddle flap. It has a short sweat-flap, or under-flap, between the panel and the girth tabs. A half panel reaches halfway down the saddle flap, and has a much larger sweat-flap. Half panelled saddles are particularly useful for younger riders because they enable a rider's knee and lower leg to get closer to the horse's or pony's sides.

Three types of linings are used on full panel and half panel saddles. Serge linings are absorbent, but they are also difficult to keep clean, and not very hard wearing. Linen, on the other hand, wears longer, dries quickly, and is easier to keep clean. The best lining material, however, is leather, which is easy to clean and has excellent wearing properties.

What are the main parts of a saddle called?

It is important to be able to name the parts of a saddle, and the following three diagrams will help you to memorise them more easily.

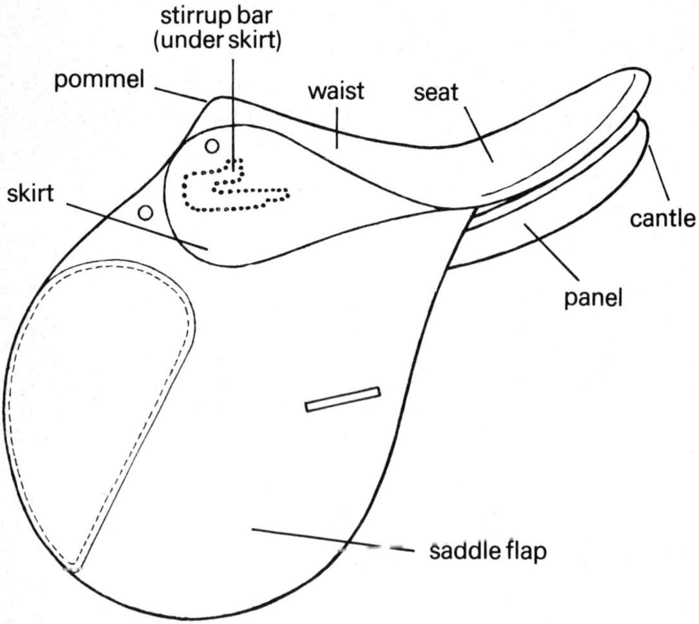

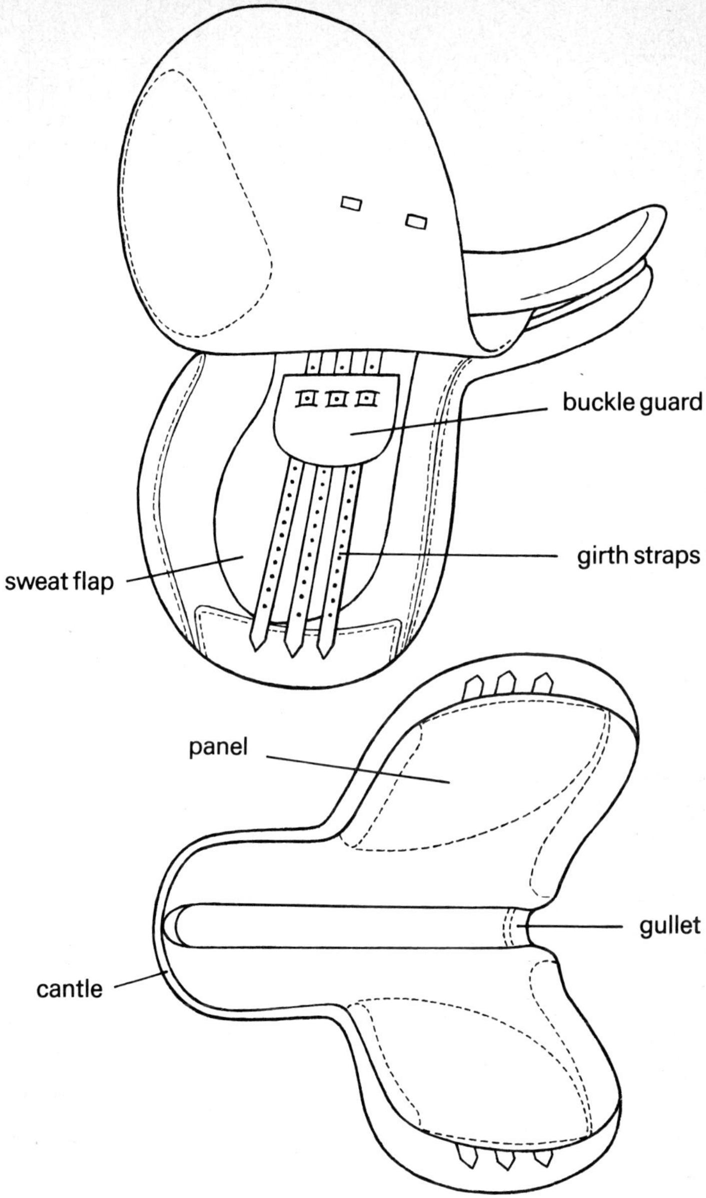
buckle guard
girth straps
sweat flap
panel
gullet
cantle

How should a saddle be fitted?

Great care must be taken to ensure that the saddle fits the horse properly. There must not be any pressure on the horse's spine, and when the rider is mounted, check the area of the cantle at the rear of the saddle. There should not be any weight on the horse's loins, and the weight of the saddle must be evenly distributed on the muscles which cover the upper part of the horse's rib cage. A badly fitting saddle can cause problems which will lay a horse or pony up for some considerable time.

It is also important to make sure that the pommel, or front of the saddle, does not press down on the horse's withers because the front arch is either too wide or too low, or pinch the withers because the arch is too narrow.

Every saddle needs checking at least once a year by the saddler who will test all the stitching and re-stuff the panels if necessary. If you are worried as to whether the saddle is pinching, use a foam numnah, and get the saddle checked by an expert as quickly as possible.

Obviously it is important to ensure that the saddle is not so large that it can hamper the play of the shoulder blades; or so small that it will be uncomfortable for the rider. Jockeys sometimes have to use very small and light saddles, but they are only in them for a short space of time.

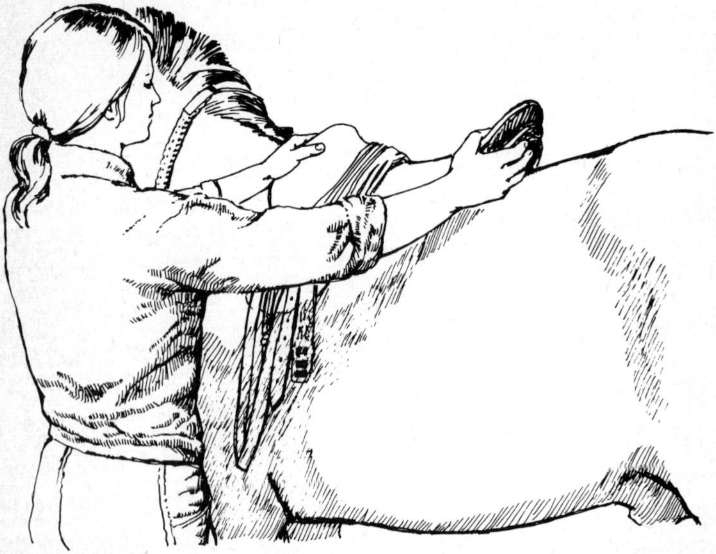

How should a saddle be handled?

Saddles can become damaged through bad and thoughtless treatment, and it is important to know how to handle them correctly.

When a saddle is being placed on the ground it should be stood on its front arch, with the girth folded across the seat, dirty side upwards. In this way the pommel can be protected from any rough hard surface. Make sure it can't be knocked over because the leather covering on the saddle can easily become torn or scratched.

Always remember to carry the saddle either along the thigh with your hand in the front arch; or with the arch in the crook of the elbow, so that the bridle can be carried on the same shoulder, out of the way of the ground, leaving your other hand free for opening the stable or tack room doors.

What are the best types of girth?

There are four main types of girth – string, nylon, web and leather – and by far the most popular are the string and leather varieties.

Web girths Rarely used nowadays because they can snap without warning, and they do not wear very well. They are also difficult to clean so that they remain looking smart. Single web girths should never be used because of their tendency to break.

String girths These have a number of good features. They last well and are easy to clean. They are less likely to slip on an unclipped horse and, more important, they help prevent galling, because air can get through between the strands of string that go to make up the body of the girth.

Nylon girths Rather like string girths, but they tend to stretch and slip more easily.

Leather girths Excellent providing they are kept clean and supple. They are usually made up of three-fold leather, and a simple way of keeping the leather soft is to put a strip of well-oiled cloth out of sight between the folds.

Girths should be of the correct length for the saddle and the horse. It is important to ensure that there are at least two spare holes above the buckle on each side when the saddle is in place, because girths usually need to be tightened once the rider has been in the saddle for a few moments and the horse has stopped blowing himself out.

web girths

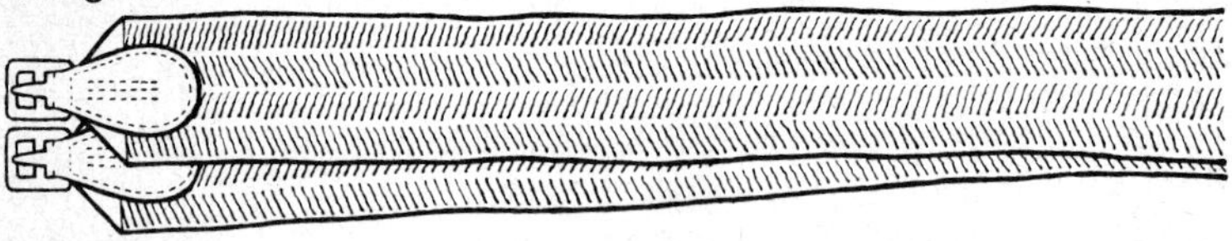

nylon girth

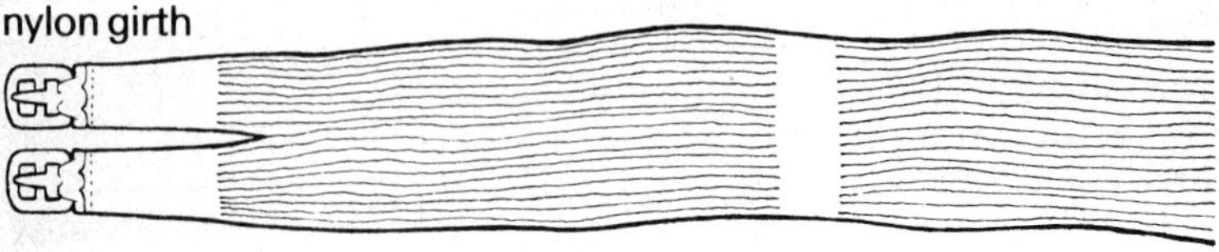

leather girth

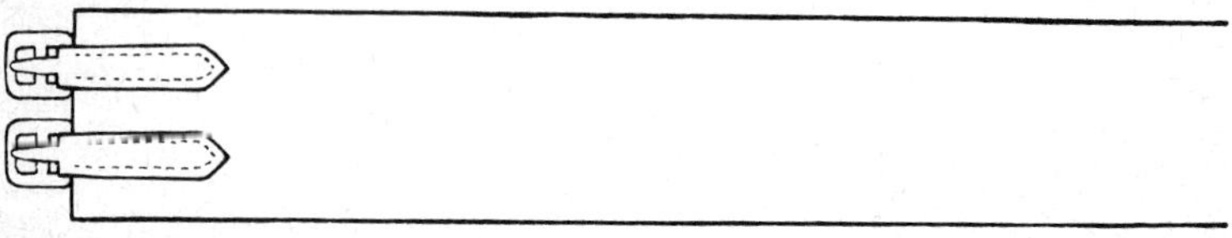

This safety stirrup is useful for very young riders.

What are the best stirrup irons?

It is most important to make certain the stirrup irons are always of best quality metal. Never buy irons made of pure nickel, because the metal is soft and the irons can bend. Steel is the safest and irons made of hand-forged stainless steel are probably the best you can buy.

Stirrup irons should never be too small for the rider's boot, and at least a centimetre (half an inch) of freedom between either side of the boot and the sides of the stirrup is essential for safety.

Some young riders use safety stirrups which have a rubber band along one side. There are varying opinions on whether the section with the rubber band should be worn on the inside, to prevent the band from becoming undone if a twig or branch gets between the stirrup and the boot, or on the outside to prevent the rider's ankle from turning inwards.

They are not entirely satisfactory and do not hang straight because they are obviously heavier on one side than the other. It is, however, important that the metal used is of the best because of this weakness.

Which bridle?

Careful attention must be paid to the bridle and also to the type and size of bit to be used, if the horse and rider are to enjoy each other's company.

The bridle is divided into several parts and it is important to learn the names of each part by heart. The following diagrams will help you to do so.

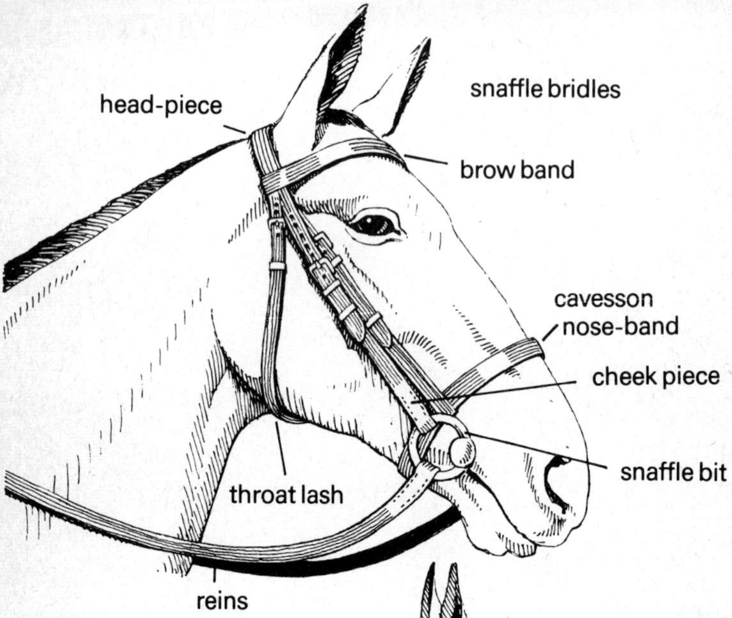

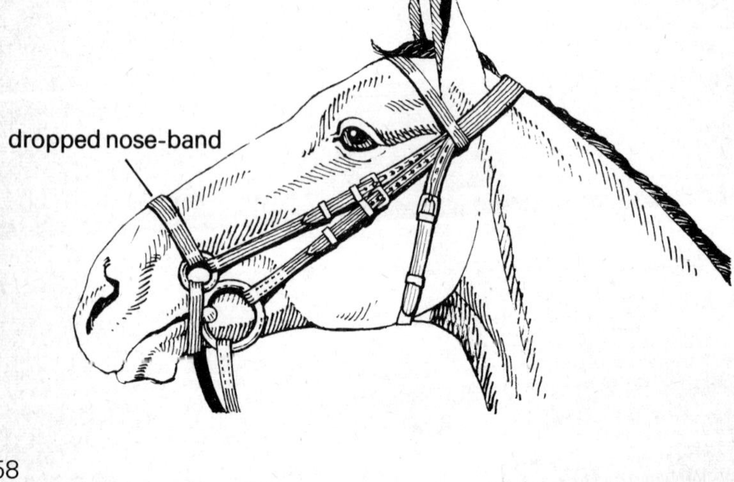

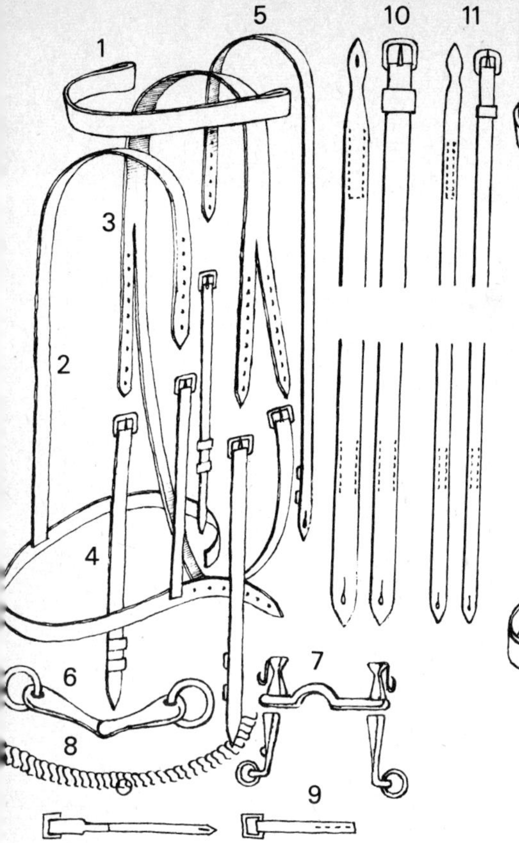

1 brow band
2 nose-band
3 head-piece
4 cheek pieces
5 bridoon cheek and sliphead
6 bridoon (snaffle) bit
7 Weymouth (curb) bit
8 curb chain
9 lip strap
10 snaffle reins
11 curb reins

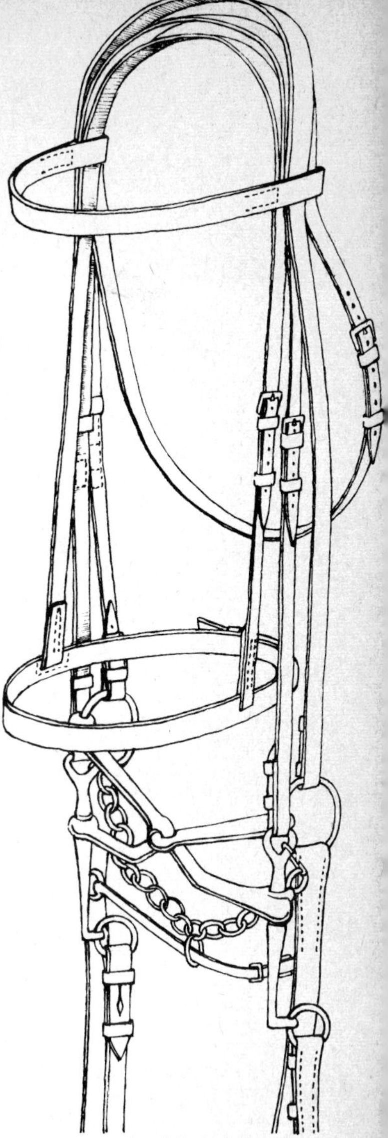

double bridle

The golden rule to remember with all forms of 'tack' is the plainer the better. Never do away with a workmanlike appearance for the sake of anything that is flashy or gaudy.

There are various bits in common use, but the four main types are the *snaffle, kimblewick, pelham* and the *double*. The snaffle

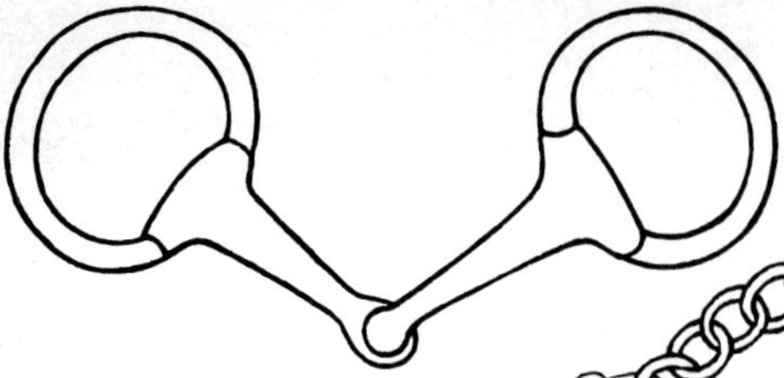

eggbutt snaffle bit

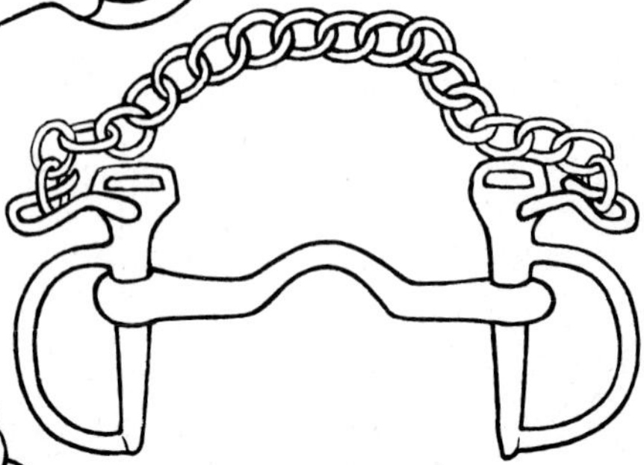

Kimblewick bit

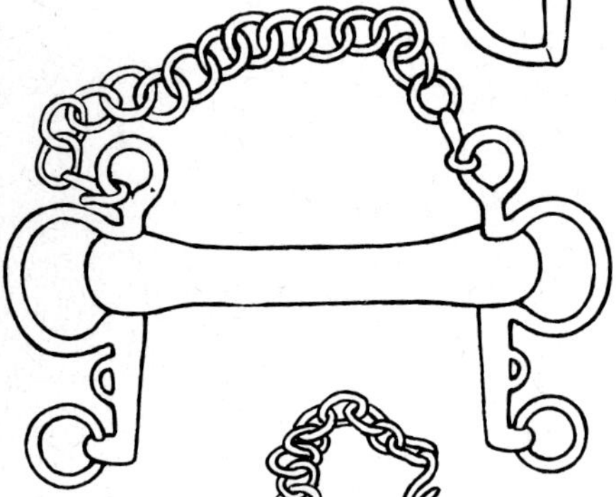

Pelham bit

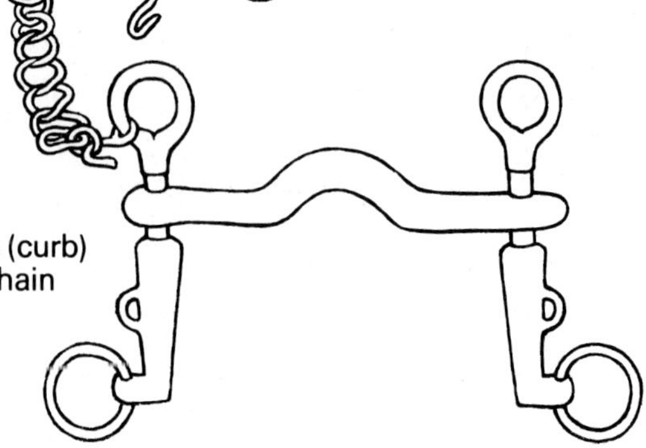

Weymouth (curb) bit and chain

and kimblewick are both used with single reins, and the pelham and the double bridle both need double reins which make them less suitable for the novice.

There are types of *bitless bridles* which, as their name suggests, means that they don't use a bit at all. They are useful if a horse has an injury to its mouth, or in some cases when a horse or pony has a particularly tender mouth, but great care must be taken in their use, and to ensure that they are fitted correctly.

Take a good look at these four types of bit and memorise the differences between them.

How should a bridle be fitted?

Care should be taken before setting off on a ride to make sure that all the parts of the bridle and the bit are fitting properly. When a bridle has been cleaned the buckles are not always replaced in the correct holes, and a badly fitting bridle is sure to lead to trouble.

The *throat lash* should never be tight. It is there to make sure that the bridle does not slip over the horse's head, but a tight throat lash, or throat latch as it is sometimes called, will interfere with a horse's breathing and its ability to flex its head.

The *brow band* must not touch the ears but should lie evenly below them. Its purpose is to prevent the head-piece from slipping back, and so the length of the brow band is important, because if it is either too long or too short the head-piece will not hang correctly.

The *cavesson nose-band* should be big enough and loose enough to allow the horse to open his mouth and flex his jaw. It should lie about half-way between the bottom of the cheek-bone and the corners of the mouth, and allow two fingers breadth between the nose-band and the front of the horse's face. A standing martingale or a lead rein is sometimes fastened to the cavesson nose-band.

The *dropped nose-band* has become very popular because it can be adjusted to prevent a horse from crossing his jaw or opening his mouth wide. Care must be taken however to make sure that it is not too tight to prevent the jaw from being flexed, and the front of the nose-band must be well above the nostrils, with the rear part fitting into the chin groove.

The *bit* should not be high enough to wrinkle the lips, and should be sufficiently wide not to pinch. If it is too wide, however, it can bruise the sides of the mouth by moving from side to side. When a double bridle is being fitted the *bridoon* should be above the bit.

The *curb chain* should lie flat in the chin groove. It should first be linked at one end over the offside hook. Then from the nearside the chain should be twisted to the right until all the links fall into place, and the chain becomes flat. Place the base of the end link on the near-side hook with the thumb uppermost, and then the link required for the correct fitting can be placed over the hook with the thumb underneath. Check that the curb chain comes into play when the cheeks of the bit are drawn back at 45 degrees to the angle of the mouth.

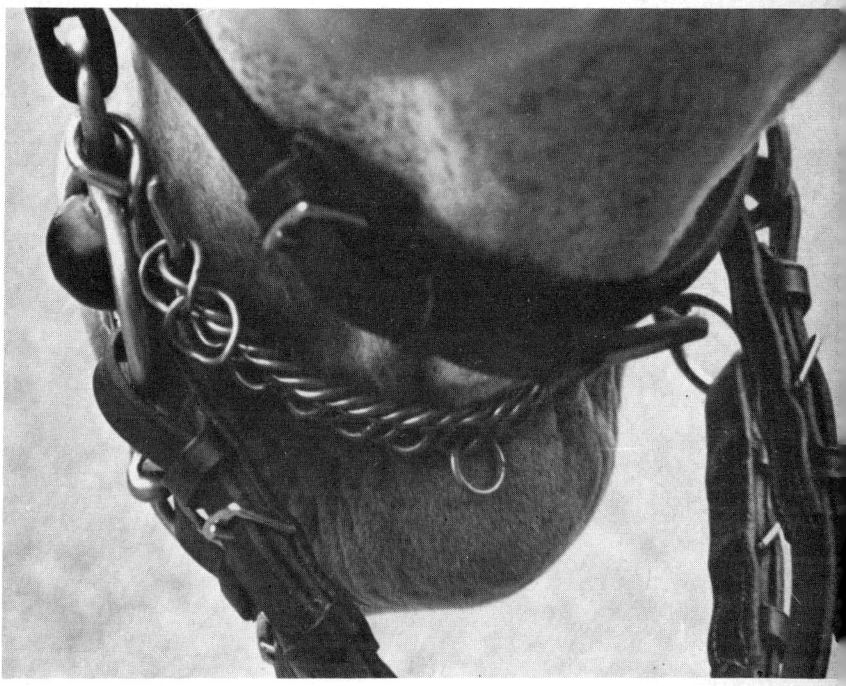

The curb chain must lie flat along the chin groove.

Left: The grakle noseband must be carefully fitted with a snaffle bit.

The *lip strap* does not need to be tight, but it must pass through the link provided for it on the curb chain. It is there to hold the chain if, for any reason, it becomes unhooked.

After checking the pieces of the bridle and the correct fitting of the bit, run your fingers under the head-pieces to make sure that they are not twisted and that the mane is lying flat.

What are martingales?

There are three types of martingale in regular use:

The standing martingale Used to prevent the horse from carrying his head too high for the rider to control him properly. It must never be used with a dropped nose-band, but the loop of the strap is attached at one end to the cavesson nose-band, and the other end passes between the horse's legs and is held in place by the girth. It can be adjusted to give the correct freedom of movement.

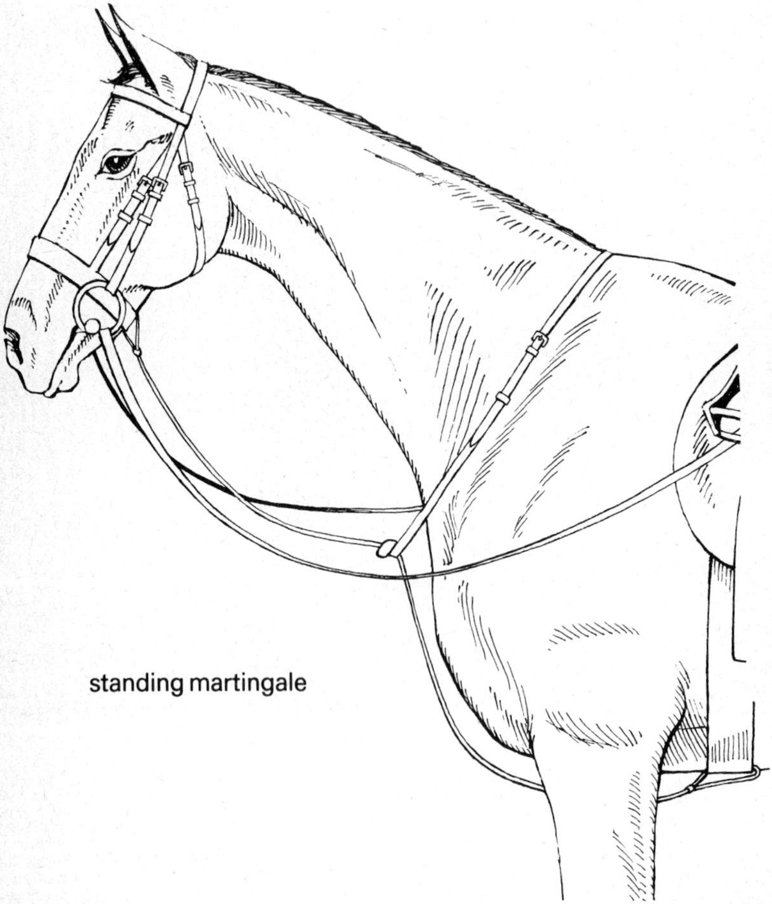

standing martingale

The running martingale Another artificial aid to prevent the horse from carrying his head too high, but while one end is still attached to the girth, the other divides into two straps each with a ring which fits over the reins. Both martingales are supported by a neck strap, but in the case of the running martingale rubber or leather straps are used on the reins to prevent the rings from becoming entangled with the bit.

The Irish martingale This looks rather like a pair of spectacles. It consists of a short strap with a ring at either end. The snaffle rein passes through the rings, beneath the horse's head, and prevents the reins from going over the head. An Irish martingale makes it impossible for both reins to end up on one side of the horse.

How should tack be looked after?

All saddlery is expensive and requires regular cleaning. While doing this, it is as well to check that all the stitching is firm, and that the bits are smooth, and do not have any sharp edges or protrusions which could cause a sore mouth.

Tack cleaning can be an enjoyable job, and if the weather is fine there is no reason why it can't be done in the open air, providing you have somewhere to hang the bridle, and something to act as a saddle-horse.

Properly cleaned and well fitting saddlery not only adds to the appearance of a horse, it also makes the rider feel more comfortable.

Leather in particular gets dry and will crack unless it is kept pliable. Castor oil, dubbin, olive oil, glycerine and neatsfoot oil are all good for leather, but good quality saddle soap contains the necessary amount of suitable ingredients to keep saddlery in good order. Never use linseed or mineral oil because it will become too hard. If saddlery has to be stored, give it a good going over with Vaseline, which will not dry or become decomposed on exposure to the air.

Never use hot water or soda and never try to dry leather too quickly.

The following materials are useful for a cleaning session depending on what sort of tack you are using.

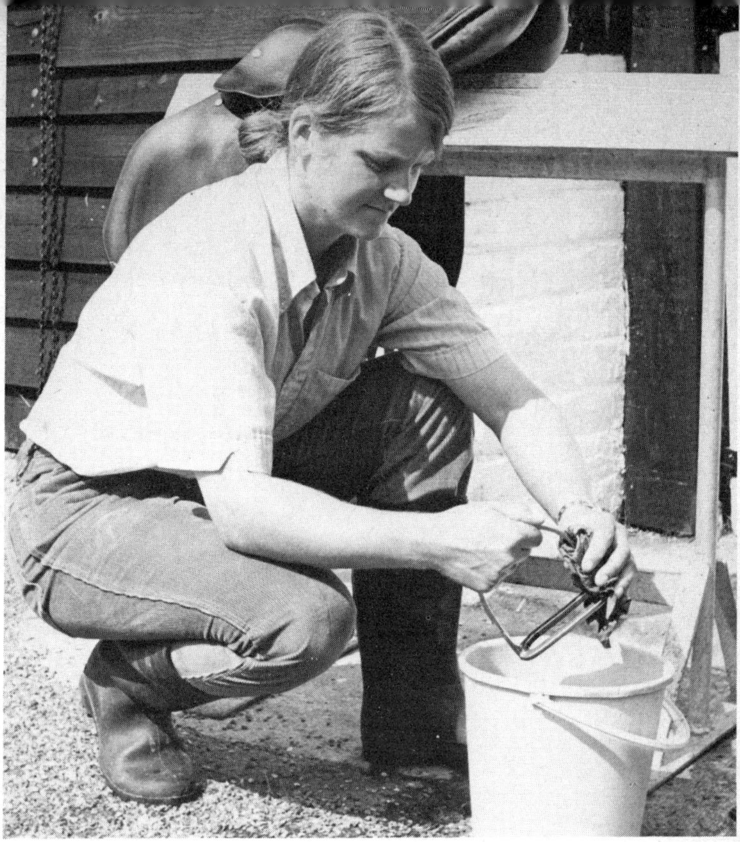

In fine weather tack can be cleaned out of doors.

1 Two sponges, one for washing over the tack and the other, a smaller sponge, for putting saddle soap on the leather.
2 A leather for drying.
3 A bar or tin of saddle soap.
4 A stable rubber or other large cloth for drying the bits and stirrup irons.
5 Some metal polish with a cloth for putting it on, and a duster for polishing it off.
6 A dandy brush for cleaning the sweat from serge linings or web girths.
7 A sharp pointed instrument for cleaning curb hooks and the D's of lip straps.
8 A bucket of warm water.

First place the saddle on a saddle-horse and remove the girths, stirrup leathers and irons, and the girth buckle guards.

The lining is the first part to be cleaned. If it is made of linen, either sponge or scrub off all the dirt and scurf, and stand the saddle up to dry. A serge lining needs to be dried and then given a thorough brushing with a dandy brush. A leather lining is more easily cleaned by holding the saddle pommel down over a bucket of cold or warm water, and rubbing it clean with a sponge. It can be

Regular saddle soaping is important to keep a saddle supple.

dried with a chamois leather, and then gone over with saddle soap.

After the saddle has been put back on to the saddle-horse it needs to be thoroughly washed with plain water, including outside and underneath the flaps. It can then be dried with a damp leather and liberally coated with saddle soap. The soap should be put on with a circular movement until it becomes absorbed into the leather.

The same should be done with the girths and stirrup leathers and the girth buckle guards.

Web, string and nylon girths need brushing daily. They can be washed occasionally with soap and water and a weak solution of ammonia. Leather girths can be washed and saddle-soaped.

The stirrup irons also need to be washed thoroughly and polished with metal polish, or silver sand in the case of plain steel.

All the buckles should also be cleaned with metal polish, but before the saddle is used again the seat and outside flaps should be rubbed over with a moist sponge and dried off with the leather. This will prevent dust, or any surplus soap, from dirtying the rider's breeches.

The bridle and other items of saddlery like the martingale have to be taken to pieces and cleaned thoroughly. Hang up the bridle on a hook. Remove the curb chain and the bit and put them into a bucket of water. Clean, dry and then polish them thoroughly. Metal polish can be used, but steel bits will need to be burnished.

After the bridle and the martingale, if one is being used, have been taken to pieces, wash the leather thoroughly with a sponge, and then dry with a damp chamois leather. Then saddle-soap all the pieces with a sponge and put the bridle together again, making sure that the buckles are in their proper places, and the strap ends are placed in their keepers and runners. Remember that keepers are the stitched loops and runners are the loops that can slide freely up and down the straps.

Finally put the throat lash through the ends of the reins and put the nose-band right round the outside of the cheek-pieces. If there is a curb chain, twist it flat and hook it round the front of the bit.

Then hang the bridle up on to the bridle hanger, which should be screwed to the tack room wall, and place the saddle on the saddle peg or saddle rack alongside. The stirrup irons should be hung underneath, and the girths, stirrup leathers and martingale should be hung alongside.

Always clean tack thoroughly after use, so that it will be clean and ready to do justice to you, and your horse, when you set out on your next ride.

Glossary

Bandages These are used on the legs and tail, mainly as a protection.
Barns Various types of barn are used for the storage of hay and straw. In America the word can refer to a stable.
Bedding This may consist of straw, sawdust, wood shavings, peat, dried bracken or shredded paper.
Bit The bit, which forms part of the bridle, is used to regulate the pace and direction of the horse, and to raise, lower and draw in the position of the head.
Bitless bridle Sometimes known as a hackamore, this is a bridle without a bit, which acts on the chin and nose carriage.
Bog spavin A puffy swelling on the inside and slightly to the front of the hock.
Bone spavin A bony growth below the hock joint.
Bridle A bridle is used to help control the movements of a horse by exerting pressure on various parts of the horse's head. These include the lips or corners of the mouth, the tongue, the bars of the mouth, the curb groove, the nose, the poll and the roof. There are six main types of bridle, the snaffle, double bridle, pelham, kimblewick, gag and bitless.
Bridoon A small snaffle bit used with a double bridle.
Bruised soles Bruised soles are usually caused by a stone and may result in temporary lameness. The sole becomes tender and may show a red mark.
Brushing boots These are usually made of leather or felt with a padded portion running down the inside of the boot to protect the joints if a horse strikes one leg with another.
Capped hock This is a swelling on the joint of the hock usually caused by shortage of bedding or injury when travelling.
Cavesson This word can either mean a cavesson nose-band which forms part of the bridle or a breaking-in cavesson which is a form of headcollar with a padded nose piece.
Clenches This is a term used to describe any protrusion of the nails holding the shoe on to the hoof.
Clipping This describes the removal of part or all of a horse's coat in the winter to enable the horse to cool and dry more quickly after fast work. There are various types of clip including the full clip, hunter clip, blanket clip and trace high clip.
Colic This is a painful disease of the digestive organs.
Condition A term used for the looks and health of a horse or pony.

Corns These are discolourations of the sole of the foot in the region of the heel, usually caused through undue pressure by a shoe.
Cracked heels An inflammation of the skin in the hollow of the heel.
Curb chain A chain which lies in the groove of the jaw just above the lower lip when fitted to a curb or pelham bit.
Day rug Usually of wool with the owner's initials in the corner and with a fillet string which passes beneath the tail and just above the hock to prevent the rug from blowing in the wind.
Double bridle A weymouth or double bridle has an additional pair of reins as well as an extra head strap and cheek-piece, to which is fastened a bridoon.
Dressage A series of gymnastic exercises to show the obedience of the horse to its rider's aids and commands.
Droppings The term usually used to refer to a horse's dung.
Dropped nose-band A nose-band which assists the action of a snaffle bit and prevents a horse from opening its mouth too wide or the bit from sliding to one side.
Electuary The name given to a medicine in which the drugs are made into a paste with a base of treacle or honey, usually used for sore throats.
Fodder The term fodder, or forage, is used to describe any foodstuff normally fed to horses.
Fodder room A room used for the storage of a horse's food, usually kept in sacks or bins.
Forging This is when the hind shoe strikes the fore shoe when a horse is trotting, usually when it is uncollected or being ridden in a slovenly manner. It can also refer to the making of a horse shoe.
Frog This is a V-shaped formation in the sole of the foot.
Gag This is a bit which has rounded leather cheek-pieces passing through the holes in a bit ring for the principal purpose of raising the horse's head.
Gig A two-wheeled carriage to seat two people.
Girth A wide band made of leather, nylon, string or web, used to hold the saddle in place. The name is also used to describe the circumference of a horse's body.
Girth gall A troublesome sore in the area of the girth.
Grazing This is used to describe horses or ponies which are feeding on grass.
Groom Someone who looks after the welfare of the horse.
Grooming The act of getting a horse or pony clean.
Hackamore A type of bitless bridle.

Hand The measurement by which the height of a horse or pony is calculated – 10 cm (4 inches).
Hay net A thick corded net in which a horse's ration of hay is placed and then hung from a ring in the stable or box.
Headcollar Used for leading an unbridled horse or pony or for tying up in a stable or stall.
Hogging A term used for removing the mane.
Hoof The horny covering of the foot from the coronet downwards.
Hoof pick A steel implement for removing dirt and stones from the hoof.
Horse blanket A thick blanket used under a night rug in cold weather.
Horse box Motor vehicle designed for transportation of horses.
Horse trailer An enclosed trailer to carry one, two or three horses, usually towed by a Land Rover or car.
Kimblewick A straight bit with a short cheek-piece and curb chain used with a single rein.
Knee-caps A felt covering to protect the horse's knees during working exercises or when travelling.
Knee spavin A bony growth at the back of the knee.
Laminitis Inflammation or fever of the feet, usually caused by fast work on hard ground or too much heating food without enough exercise.
Lip strap A thin leather strap which holds the curb chain in place.
Loose box Form of stabling which gives freedom of movement.
Manger A feed container usually made of iron or hardwood and fastened to the wall of a stable or stall at a suitable height.
Martingale A leather device to regulate the horse's head carriage. There are three main types – standing, running and Irish.
Mounting block A low platform on which a rider stands when mounting a horse.
Mud fever Inflammation of the heels, legs or belly.
Mucking out The process of cleaning a horse box or stall and removing the droppings.
Muck-heap The name frequently given to a manure heap.
Navicular A disease of the navicular bone, usually confined to the forefeet.
New Zealand rug A weather-proof canvas rug, usually used on horses turned out in winter.
Night rug A jute rug, partly or fully lined, used to keep horses warm at night.
Over-reaching When the toe of the hind shoe strikes against the

heel of the forefeet.

Over-reach boot A circular rubber boot used to prevent injury to the coronet when a horse over-reaches.

Paddock An enclosed area of grassland used for grazing horses or ponies.

Pelham A bit with a double rein and curb chain designed to do the work of a double bridle.

Pincers An instrument used by a blacksmith.

Plaiting The process of putting plaits into a horse's mane or tail to improve the appearance.

Pritchel A pointed metal tool used by a blacksmith to carry a hot shoe.

Puller A horse which pulls, usually through having had its mouth ruined.

Pulled mane or tail When the hair from the underneath of the mane or the side of the dock is removed by pulling to give a tidy effect.

Pulse A horse's pulse is normally 36 to 40 beats to the minute. It is usually taken at the submaxillary artery under the jaw.

Roadwork Exercising a horse on the road to get it fit.

Roller A form of girth made of leather, webbing or hemp to keep a rug in place.

Rugging up A term used for putting rugs on a horse.

Saddle Usually made of felt or leather, attached to the horse's back by a girth to provide support for the rider.

Saddle-horse A wooden stand upon which saddles can be placed for cleaning or storage.

Saddle soap A specially prepared soap which is applied with a damp sponge for cleaning saddles, bridles and other leather harness.

Saddle-tree A frame upon which a saddle is built.

Shoeing The art of making and fixing a shoe on to a horse's foot.

Side bone A hard lump on the coronet on either side of the heel.

Side reins Reins attached to the roller for training purposes or when lunging a young horse.

Side saddle A saddle, usually used by women, when the rider sits sideways on a horse.

Skip A wicker-type basket or metal container used to collect droppings in a stable.

Snaffle fit A bit needing only one rein, which usually consists of a single-jointed or unjointed mouth piece.

Splint A small bony growth between the splint bone and the canon bone.

Stall A compartment for a horse in a stable in which a horse must be tied.
Stirrup iron A metal fitting in which the rider's foot is placed.
Stirrup leathers Leather straps which are used to attach the stirrup irons to the saddle.
Summer sheet Usually made of cotton or linen to keep away flies and dust from a horse's coat in summer.
Sweat sheet A rug, rather like a string vest, which is used to help cool a horse when hot.
Sweet itch An irritable condition of the skin at the crest, withers and croup in summer.
Tack The name given to describe the saddlery used on a horse or pony.
Tack room A room used for the storage of saddlery.
Tail guard Made of leather or felt and covers the dock completely to prevent any damage to the tail when the horse is travelling.
Temperature The normal temperature of a horse is 38°C (100·5°F).
Tendons Fibrous structures forming bands and cords attaching the muscles to the bones of the legs.
Tendon boots Specially designed boots, usually of leather, which protect the tendons.
Tooth rasp A special file for removing the sharp edges of a horse's teeth.
Trimming Tidying the hairs of a horse's head, mane and tail.
Wisp A pad made of rope, hay or straw, used for toning up a horse's skin.
Wither pad A pad made of soft material placed under the saddle to prevent undue pressure on a horse's back, particularly when the saddle does not fit well.
Wolf teeth Rudimentary teeth in front of the upper and lower molar teeth.
Worms Parasites which can affect the condition of a horse.
Warbles Lumps in the region of the saddle caused by the warble fly.

Other horse and pony books by the same authors

Robert Owen

My Learn to Ride Book Illustrated in colour throughout, this is an informative book aimed at giving younger people an all-round introduction to horsemanship.

Successful Riding and Jumping The techniques necessary to develop the skills of riding and jumping successfully are clearly described.

John Bullock

Horse and Pony Quiz Book Specially written for horse lovers of all ages, this book gives an enormous amount of information on the care and enjoyment of the horse.

Robert Owen and John Bullock

The Horse and Pony Gift Book A big book, packed with facts about horse care and health, breeds, training, buying, the work of the farrier, gymkhanas, riding holidays, show jumping and all the equestrian sports. Illustrated throughout in black and white and colour.

Young Riders Guides

Buying and Keeping a Horse or Pony
Caring for a Horse or Pony
Riding and Schooling
All about Jumping

More Beaver Books

We hope you have enjoyed this Beaver Book. Here are some of the other titles:

Ghost Horse Dramatic story about a legendary stallion in the American West, by Joseph E. Chipperfield

My Favourite Horse Stories Dorian Williams has chosen fifteen of his favourite stories and poems about horses; a collection to delight all animal lovers

Lord of the Forest Written by 'BB' and with beautiful illustrations by Denys Watkins-Pitchford, this is the story of a mighty oak from its planting in 1272 until the last acorn from the dead tree is replanted in the 1939–45 war. A magnificent panorama of nature and history

The Call of the Wild The epic story of Buck the great sledge dog in the frozen North, by Jack London

Who Knows? Twelve unsolved mysteries involving sudden death, mysterious disappearances and hidden treasure, by Jacynth Hope-Simpson

The Tail of the Trinosaur Charles Causley's splendidly funny verse story about a prehistoric beast which comes to England from the Amazon jungle, with illustrations by Jill Gardiner

New Beavers are published every month and if you would like the *Beaver Bulletin* – which gives all the details – please send a stamped addressed envelope to:

Beaver Bulletin
The Hamlyn Group
Astronaut House
Feltham
Middlesex TW14 9AR

381994